G000070355

About the Author

Peter Bolt is a management consultant, mentor, coach and business strategist. He founded The Bolt Consultancy in 1988 and his client list includes notable blue-chip companies as well as various organisations of different shapes and sizes.

Peter has presented several public lectures and seminars, including his "Masterclass in Management" at the Institute of Directors, as well as in-house with numerous companies and local authorities. He is a member of the Institute of Directors and the Marketing Society.

Peter's first book, *The Whole Manager: Achieving Success Without Selling Your Soul*, was a critical and commercial success and is now in its second printing.

He is married, with a film producer son and an actress daughter. He and his wife divide their time between London and Herefordshire.

Coaching for Growth

How to Bring Out the Best in Your Team and Yourself

Peter Bolt

Author of *The Whole Manager*

Oak Tree Press

Dublin

Oak Tree Press
Merrion Building
Lower Merrion Street
Dublin 2, Ireland
www.oaktreepress.com

© 2000 Peter Bolt

A catalogue record of this book is
available from the British Library.

Hardback ISBN 1 86076 169 0
Paperback ISBN 1 86076 182 8

All rights reserved. No part of this publication may be re-
produced or transmitted in any form or by any means, including photocopying and recording, without written permission of the publisher. Such written permission must also
be obtained before any part of this publication is stored in a
retrieval system of any nature. Requests for permission
should be directed to Oak Tree Press, Merrion Building,
Lower Merrion Street, Dublin 2, Ireland.

Printed in Britain by MPG Books
Bodmin, Cornwall

Contents

Preface

The aim of coaching is the same as that of successful management: to achieve profitable growth by making the most of an organisation's most valuable resources — its people.

Coaching is for everyone, not just the high flyers or those with a specific problem. Coaching can have a very positive impact on people's performance and careers so that both individuals and organisations benefit. More than just focusing on skills, it helps to develop mental strength and self-belief, which will help people keep going when times are tough. It is particularly appropriate for these times of rapid change.

Coaching is not a soft option. At best, the art of coaching is challenging, sometimes uncomfortable, energising and immensely satisfying. To witness how people can enhance their performance, perception and behaviour as a result of coaching can be deeply rewarding. Strong partnerships can be formed but always, without exception, the true test of coaching is how the individual being coached performs on their own. Coaching is not a leaning post!

The contents of this book focus on the prime areas of coaching but includes elements of mentoring, that special ingredient which comes with experience from those who have had plenty of knocks on the way up. In addition, the book deals with coaching the whole person, which is essential if the process is to have long-lasting benefits.

If more organisations developed coaching as a key element of their management strategy or approach, then there would be more thriving, highly effective and well-motivated teams in organisations of all kinds.

As someone who has practised the art of coaching for many years now, I remain fascinated by its potential and the challenges it presents. I would therefore welcome any suggestions, criticisms, opinions, or other feedback from readers on the subject of coaching. I can be contacted at the address below:

Peter Bolt
12 Devonhurst Place
Chiswick, London W4 4JB
Telephone: 020-8747 0109

I look forward to hearing from you.

Chapter One

Why Coaching?

Background

Let's begin with a basic question: why coaching? Why is effective coaching the key to organisational success in the 21st century? The reason is simple: the role of managers has changed fundamentally over the last decade and a new approach to people management is essential for companies to succeed.

There once was a time when the job of managers was to supervise and control the people they managed — that is, to tell them what to do, help them to do it properly, measure their performance and reward or correct that performance as need be. Those days, however, are for the most part long gone.

Today the very nature of business is completely different from a generation ago:

- *Organisations are more decentralised*, which means that employees need to make more, and better, decisions themselves.

- *Employees are becoming more empowered*, which means that they are more involved in the organisation and don't expect to simply carry out instructions.

- *Competition and globalisation have increased*, which means that organisations need to get higher quality performance from their people.

- *Change is rapid and continuous*, which means that employees need to be flexible and adaptive.

- *There are fewer management levels in organisations*, which means that employees must be able to take on more responsibility.

- *Old career patterns no longer exist*, which means that employees must adopt a different attitude towards issues of security and advancement.

- *Increasingly, new technologies and work processes are being adopted*, which means that employees must embrace continual learning.

- *Innovation and rapid response to market place changes can be the key to success*, which means that employees must be committed to improvement and new ideas.

- *In general, work pressures are greater than ever*, which means that organisations need to provide more and better support for their employees if they are to perform effectively.

Added to the above is the fact that information technology has had a huge impact on how we do business. High quality decisions must be made and communicated much more rapidly than ever before, which increases pressure at all levels of the organisation. As we will show throughout this book, coaching offers a very effective way of helping both individuals and organisations deal with these new realities in the workplace.

People are clearly an organisation's most important asset, but just hiring the best is not enough. Managers must find effective ways to support their staff, to remove obstacles which may be holding them back and help them to develop their full potential. Coaching is the answer.

As you read this book, you will come across my Ten Commandments of Coaching (see Chapter 12 for the complete list). Here is the first:

> ### Commandment Number One:
>
> *Stop just managing — Coaching is the key to success in today's organisations.*

Coaching Defined

Coaching is a participative partnership designed to develop an individual to their full potential. It is a one-to-one process which typically focuses on personal development and problem-solving, whereby the coach and individual agree on the issues involved and jointly consider solutions. Whereas the individual being coached must accept responsibility for the decisions being taken, a good coach will be able to provide essential support and feedback along the way. As an external observer, the coach brings a fresh perspective on the issues involved in a safe, non-threatening environment.

In the next chapter we'll look at some specific issues and problems that can be addressed by coaching, but in general terms coaching can help individuals:

- Become more aware of their strengths and weaknesses, and how to build on the former and alleviate the latter

- Establish specific and realisable business and personal objectives

- Feel like an integral and valued member of the team who can express their views freely

- Deal with difficult or stressful situations, such as major work changes, personal problems or other challenges

- Improve communication skills and understand how to work better with others to get things done.

The overall impact is to create an enhanced self-confidence, which becomes the bedrock of ongoing development and success.

Coaching normally occurs between an individual and their direct manager or some other senior person in the organisation, though as we will see later, coaching can also be effective in other situations. In addition, coaching is not only applicable in the workplace but can be beneficial in the family, the community and elsewhere.

There is an obvious connection between coaching in sports and in the workplace. Just as an athlete benefits considerably from the expertise and attention of a personal coach, so too does an employee benefit from coaching at work. In both cases, goals are clearly defined, performance can be measured and improved, and feedback is frequent and constructive. And in both cases, ultimately the quality of the performance is up to the individual alone, with the coach providing support and encouragement.

What Coaching is Not

Coaching is not just another form of management or supervision. As we will see, the key to successful coaching lies in the individual's willingness and ability to identify their own abilities or shortcomings and to take action as needed. The coach cannot just tell the person what to do, nor can the individual become too reliant on the coach's views and suggestions. The individual must be an active participant in the process at all times and accept ultimate responsibility.

Coaching is also different from training, mentoring, counselling, performance correction and other forms of one-to-one interaction. *Training* tends to involve specific skills, whereby the individual is a passive recipient in the process. With a *mentor*, the individual is explicitly learning from a more experienced senior person who typically advises on career advancement issues. The relationship is not one of an equal partnership and often dependency can result. An exception would be the mentor–coach, which will be discussed later, where a coach is dealing with more senior executives. *Counselling* tends to focus on certain personal difficulties affecting performance, while *performance correction* clearly addresses specific shortcomings and is related to a disciplinary process. Only coaching focuses on a collaborative partnership that emphasises personal development and problem-solving, and only coaching can help to create the whole manager that is needed in today's organisations.

Benefits of Coaching

Many of the benefits of coaching would seem self-apparent, but it may be useful here to cite the key ones for all involved.

Benefits for the Individual

- Receive personalised, one-to-one support focusing on individual strengths and weaknesses

- Be able to ask questions, express views and voice concerns in a safe environment

- Have a sounding board for new ideas and suggestions

- Deal with specific problems or a general lack of confidence

- Identify personal and organisational goals and the steps needed to realise them

- Manage their career and personal development

- Work on shortcomings or problems in a non-judgemental setting

- Feel valued and trusted in the organisation, also more involved

- Get help in simplifying life, for example, the balance between work and home pressures.

Benefits to Coach

- Effective way of improving performance and bringing out the best in each individual

- Makes individuals more responsible and less dependent on their manager; able to solve problems on their own

- Shared responsibility reduces burden on coach or manager

- Increases understanding of individual strengths and weaknesses

- More effective method of evaluating employee performance

- Get feedback on own abilities and shortcomings as a manager

- Personal satisfaction of helping individuals grow to their full potential.

Benefits to the Organisation

- Creates a learning environment that leads to continual improvement

- Increases innovation, productivity, creativity and communication in all sectors of the organisation

- Offers cost-effective personalised development

- Fosters initiative and commitment throughout the organisation

- Provides an effective way to implement major change programmes in the organisation

- Helps to identify problems before they become crises

- Demonstrates management commitment to staff, which leads to increased loyalty.

Table 1 below highlights the differences between the traditional organisation and the coaching-based organisation.

Table 1: Traditional Organisation vs Coaching-based Organisation

Traditional Organisation	Coaching-based Organisation
Hierarchical	Decentralised
Top–down management	Empowered staff
Command-and-control	Collaborative
Rigid and inflexible	Innovative
Learning is stifled	Learning is encouraged
Risk-averse	Entrepreneurial
Annual performance appraisals	Ongoing performance assessment
Training via courses	Training via coaching
Resists change	Responds quickly to change
Little loyalty in staff	Committed and loyal staff
Loses best people	Attracts and keeps quality people

Plan of the Book

This book is designed to give the reader an overview of how coaching can transform and sustain any organisation and help individuals to achieve their full potential. Following this introductory chapter, **Chapter 2** looks at the fundamentals of one-to-one coaching. It describes the types of subjects covered in a coaching relationship, some of the typical goals and objectives, and looks at some of the issues appropriate to coaching.

Chapter 3 looks at what actually occurs in a coaching session and provides advice on how to get useful responses from individuals during coaching. *Chapter 4* considers the skills and attitudes necessary to become a good coach. It also looks at some of the key coaching mistakes to avoid.

Chapter 5 then discusses the various coaching styles that can be effective. There is no one way to coach, and different situations often require different approaches. *Chapter 6* looks at some of the various challenges the coach might encounter, from helping the underachiever reach their true potential to keeping the high flyer from becoming bored and restless. Other performance types are also considered.

Chapter 7 addresses the possibility of coaching downwards, sideways and upwards in the organisation. The approach and issues are different in each, as are the benefits and dangers. *Chapter 8* follows with a look at the mentor–coach, a special type of coaching that is particularly effective with senior executives.

Chapter 9 considers some specific situations, usually difficult ones, where coaching can be particularly beneficial. Organisational issues (such as downsizing, increased competition, etc.) as well as personal issues (such as health problems, substance abuse, stress, family problems, etc.) are all considered in the context of coaching. **Chapter 10** then looks at the challenge of coaching the whole person, not just the employee. Organisations are increasingly aware that getting the balance between work life and home life is crucial, and coaching can play a critical role in achieving it.

Chapter 11 argues that coaching skills are not only applicable in the organisation but can also be used with family members, friends, neighbours and others. Coaching is, in effect, for (almost) everyone.

Finally, **Chapter 12** lists my Ten Commandments of Coaching, which will help to summarise my sense of what coaching can achieve for all parties involved.

As an Appendix, I've included the transcripts of an actual coaching session (disguised to ensure confidentiality) which will help to illustrate how coaching actually works.

Chapter Two

Helping Others to Help Themselves: The Fundamentals of Coaching

Introduction

Coaching styles and approaches can vary from individual to individual but there are some fundamental rules that I think apply in all cases. This chapter will address some of these coaching basics, and then will look at how an actual coaching session should be structured. We'll look at the types of issues and problems that are typically addressed during coaching, as well as characteristic goals and objectives. Finally, we'll consider how coaches can get honest and illuminating responses from individuals by asking specific kinds of questions.

The Responsibilities of the Coach

The first rule of coaching is that it is a collaborative process and the coach's job is to act as a facilitator. The coach cannot end up solving the individual's problems for them or constantly be giving advice for them to follow slavishly. The coach's job is to help the individual understand the issues, come up with possible solutions and put them into practice, thereby becoming more effective. The coach must not, however, end up as a crutch for the individual to lean on.

I once had a client who asked to see me more than once a month, when he would produce a list of problems which we would discuss and agree a course of action. I soon realised that I was being used by him to help solve problems which he should have been thinking through on his own. He had become dependent on our coaching sessions, which was not helping his own growth at all. We discussed the problem and were able to make the sessions truly testing, collaborative and useful.

> ### Commandment Number Two:
>
> *Coaching means helping others to help themselves — if it's not a collaborative process, it's not coaching.*

In the next chapter, we will look more closely at the qualities that make up a good coach, but in general the coach should:

- Listen — and be seen to listen — very well
- Be honestly interested in the individual

- Have sound communication and negotiating skills

- Be able to build rapport with others easily

- Be adept at problem-solving

- Be patient, supportive and enthusiastic.

The Responsibilities of the Individual

Above all, the individual has a responsibility to be open about their strengths and weaknesses and be keen to change should it be needed. The process cannot work if the individual is not willing to co-operate fully with the coach. This means that they should:

- Be willing to examine all aspects of their performance and behaviour

- Be open to considering a wide range of possible courses of action

- Not get defensive about criticism or suggestions

- Take specific action as agreed during sessions

- Agree to stick with the process for an agreed length of time.

Confidentiality and Trust

Obviously, coaching will only work if there is complete trust between the coach and the individual. This means that the individual must feel free to speak without fear of being judged or of the conversation being repeated to others. These sessions are often opportunities for the individual to try out new ideas or even just to think out loud, both of which will only happen if confidentiality is guaranteed. Similarly, an honest exchange of views will only occur in an atmosphere of trust and respect. Once that trust has been lost or compromised, or if the mutual respect is no longer there, then the coaching relationship is doomed.

<u>**Commandment Number Three**</u>:

Confidentiality is key — lose their trust and the game is over.

Coaching is About Learning

At the heart of the coaching relationship is the individual's genuine desire to learn — to learn about their own strengths and weaknesses, about what they really want in their lives, about how to develop themselves and also how to overcome whatever is holding them back, about how to deal successfully with others, and so on. The coach leads the process, asks questions that help the individual to understand the issues involved, and at all times tries to build up the individual's self-confidence and positive outlook.

Enhancing Self-esteem

A key goal of coaching is to maintain or enhance the individual's self-esteem. A positive self-belief is much more likely to lead to further development and constructive change, and the coach is ideally situated to reinforce it at all times. This can take a variety of forms, from focusing on particular strengths — with specific examples — to minimising the extent or significance of perceived weaknesses. The coach needs to be honest at all times, however, and not gloss over real problems or pretend they do not exist. In fact, to do so would be seriously counterproductive, as the individual would realise that the coach is being less than sincere and the bond of trust would be broken. But at the same time, it is possible to work on areas for improvement without damaging the individual's overall self-confidence. At the end of each coaching session, the individual should emerge with *at least* as much self-esteem as when they started.

Coaching is for (Almost) Everyone

Some people mistakenly believe that coaching is only for problem employees or for dealing with specific issues. In fact, nearly everyone would benefit from coaching if they enter into it in the right frame of mind and are willing to change. It's true that coaching can be *particularly* suited to individuals working on specific goals or objectives, but each of us could find some aspect of our work or personal life that could be improved. It's also true that some people, for whatever reason, simply cannot be coached and the wise coach will realise that fact early on before spending too much time on those individuals.

I was coaching one manager whom I felt was simply not listening to me. I decided to test this by asking him to tell me which advice I gave him was particularly useful. From the splutters and silences that followed, it was clear that his mind was elsewhere. I asked him what the problem was and he said that he wasn't learning anything from me and felt that the sessions were a waste of time. We discussed it further and agreed that for whatever reason we had failed to establish any rapport and agreed to call the sessions to a halt. In this case the person's arrogance prevented him from being open to the ideas of others, but whenever there's a complete breakdown it's best to call it a day.

Coaching is Not Therapy

The purpose of coaching is to build on an individual's strengths and alleviate weaknesses, and it extends beyond the workplace into home life and elsewhere. By its very nature, it addresses attitudes, feelings, relationships and other personal areas, but it must be emphasised that it is not designed to deal with serious emotional problems. A coach needs to recognise when issues have moved beyond their own level of expertise and at that point recommend someone qualified to deal with the situation.

Typical Issues Addressed in Coaching Sessions

There are an almost endless number of subjects that can be addressed during coaching sessions. Some will deal with organisational issues, some with personal ones. Some topics will be immediate in nature while others will have a long-term focus. Below are some typical subjects that are appropriate for coaching:

- *Business Goals — "I know that we can increase productivity by 25 per cent, but how?"* Coaching sessions offer an excellent opportunity to identify different ways of doing things, new initiatives or approaches. Exploring a range of options together and discussing them in depth allows the individual to realise it is possible to tackle almost any problem or challenge.

- *Personal Growth — "I seem to be stuck in a rut and don't know how to get out."* Coaching can be particularly helpful in providing an objective view to the individual's career and personal options. The coach needs to help the individual understand, and sometimes face up to, what it is they really want, and then agree steps on how to achieve it.

- *Becoming a New Manager — "My staff just doesn't seem to be coming together as a team."* Here the coach needs to help the individual understand how they are viewed by the staff and what steps can be taken to improve team performance. It may be appropriate for the coach to give their own view of the team's perceptions and then to discuss whether they are justified and what action needs to be taken.

- *Balancing Work and Home Life — "I'm under increasing pressure at work and I'm not getting a chance to see my kids grow up."* This is an increasingly frequent subject for coaching sessions as people try to figure out how to get this balance right. Often there are issues of time management or unrealistic expectations at work involved, or possibly a bad relationship with the immediate manager (hopefully not the coach!) and possible solutions need to be considered.

- *How One is Perceived at Work — "I never get any recognition for the work I do and I don't know why."* Again, a coach can help the individual understand how they are perceived in the organisation and what steps can be taken to change that perception. This issue of "perception" is not explored enough in my view, and coaching offers an ideal opportunity to do so. It is also a good way for the coach and individual to forge a positive partnership, as the coach can observe at close range how much progress is being made.

- *New Supervisor — "We got off on the wrong foot and I don't know what to do next."* A fairly typical complaint and one ideally suited to coaching. Together the coach and the individual can devise strategies to repair this relationship.

- *Delegating Work* — *"I know I need to delegate more but it seems so much easier just to do it myself."* The coach should be able to help the individual understand why they have difficulty delegating and why they urgently need to address this problem.

- *Changing Business Environment* — *"We seem to have new pressures every day, and everything changes so fast, I don't know how to respond."* Here the coach needs to understand the nature of the problem and help the individual work through possible solutions, discussing the pros and cons of each. The coach in this case serves several functions: provides a sympathetic ear, asks appropriate and useful questions, acts as a sounding board for new ideas and offers advice on how to approach the problem.

- *Time Management* — *"There never seems to be enough time to think through the big issues."* Another typical subject for coaching sessions and one I feel is easily addressed. There are numerous time management strategies that can be used (see case example at the end of the chapter) and the coach can help the individual discover the right one that suits their situation.

- *Dealing with Change in the Organisation — "Ever since the merger, the culture here has been completely different."* Various issues involving culture change are also common subjects for coaching sessions. There are often no easy answers, but expressing the problem and considering options can be very helpful. I had one client who was involved in numerous acquisitions and noted that there was nearly always a major culture clash upon merging. We were able to talk through the issues involved, which helped to alleviate the problem.

- *Ethical Issues — "I just can't decide whether or not it's the right thing to do."* Here the coach needs to be careful as there may be legal issues involved or the decision may impact negatively on the organisation. Still, it's the coach's responsibility to help the individual to weigh up the options and arrive at the right choice, not to make it for them.

Clearly the above list is just a sample of possible subjects, but it should give the reader an idea of why coaching is particularly well suited to dealing with certain kinds of issues.

Topics not Appropriate for Coaching Sessions

While as a general rule everything under the sun should be open for discussion, there are clearly some subjects that are not appropriate for coaching sessions. In fact, the coach should underline this fact early on so that it is clear to both parties. For example, the coach is not there to help the individual get additional time off or to sort out their computer problems. Coaching is not a substitute for basic managerial or administrative tasks unless, of course, specific issues are adversely affecting job performance. In general, the coach needs to take control of the sessions to a certain extent to ensure that they are useful and relevant so that the time is not wasted.

As we will see in the next chapter, the coach simply needs to establish ground rules at the beginning of the coaching session as to what the process should be, and then deal with any inappropriate questions as they arise.

Case Example

To conclude this chapter, here is a good example of the benefits that can result from coaching. For a longer and more detailed example of coaching at work, see the case study in the appendix.

James was a very capable individual who was quickly promoted to positions of increasing responsibility. When he came to me, he had been given a major promotion and was feeling totally overwhelmed by the responsibilities of his new position. Over several sessions, we discussed exactly what the issues were and concluded that the primary problem was that the day-to-day pressures of the job prevented him from stepping back and focusing on the big picture, which, ulti-

mately, would determine his success or failure. Together we decided that at heart it was a time management issue; that is, he was failing to devote enough time to a task that was now actually fundamental to his new position: quality thinking time.

We kicked around several possible solutions and finally agreed that he would schedule three-hour quality thinking sessions every other week. He would prepare for these sessions as he would for other important meetings so that they were taken seriously and he was well prepared. He would schedule the sessions somewhere away from his office where he wouldn't be disturbed and he could concentrate. During these sessions, he would then think through the key "bigger picture" issues confronting him and his group and devise strategies to deal with them.

After four months of holding these three-hour thinking sessions, he felt on top of his job and was relatively relaxed. He told me it was the single best piece of advice he'd ever received — though in truth, we came up with it together.

Chapter Three

The Coaching Session

We will now look at what actually happens in a coaching session. Different coaches will clearly operate in different ways, but in this chapter I will describe how I think the coaching session should progress. I will first look at the initial steps involved to get the sessions off on the right foot, and I'll then describe how continuing sessions might go. I will then provide some examples of the type of questions to ask to elicit certain kinds of responses, and will conclude with a look at how to deal with resistance during coaching.

The Seven Steps

In the initial stages of a coaching relationship, it is advisable to go through the following seven steps:

1. Set the ground rules — time, place, duration, frequency, process, etc.

2. Create a supportive and safe environment — establish rapport

3. Agree on the goals and objectives

4. Analyse the current situation and come to an agreement on the key issues or any problems at hand

5. Devise an action plan

6. Gain a commitment from the individual to the action plan

7. Monitor the situation and provide feedback.

Set the Ground Rules — Time, Place, Duration, Frequency, Process, etc.

The coaching session should always take place at a location and time that is convenient for both the individual and the coach. The location should be somewhere private where they are unlikely to be disturbed or overheard. If the coach is not the individual's direct manager, it should be made clear to that person that the individual will be unavailable for two hours (or whatever the agreed duration is) and that the manager will be informed in advance of additional sessions. The coach and individual together will agree on the date and time for subsequent sessions, usually at the end of the first one. The coach will also discuss here in broad terms how the coaching sessions will work, the responsibilities of the coach and the individual, and so on.

Create a Supportive and Safe Environment — Establish Rapport

It is critical at the outset that the coach creates an environment that is conducive to a relaxed and honest exchange of views. It is best to start with a friendly chat, showing a real interest in the individual as a person, asking questions about family, background, hobbies and so on. To be effective, the coach needs to know this background information anyway, but at the beginning the goal is simply to let the individual relax and get used to the process. As we will see later, rapport is one of the key skills coaches need to develop. In fact, it is of little value to continue a coaching session unless rapport has been established between coach and individual.

It is also useful at this point to discuss in general terms the purpose of the coaching sessions. General objectives should be set out and the responsibilities of the coach — ensuring confidentiality, being supportive and non-judgemental, etc. — as well as those of the individual — honesty, willingness to change, etc. — should be explained. The atmosphere should be friendly and positive.

Agree on the Goals and Objectives

The next step is to discuss the specific issues at hand with the individual. These will obviously vary from person to person; with some there may be only a few and with others quite a list, but if possible it is useful to get them all out in the open so that the coach has as complete a picture as possible. There is often a good deal of overlap between objectives — or at least a clear pattern — but in some cases there may be quite a few disparate issues to consider. The individual should be the one to suggest the specific goals and objectives of the sessions, and there must be complete agreement between the coach and the individual before proceeding to the next step.

One of my clients asks the following five questions at the beginning of a coaching session:

1. What benefit would you like most to get out of these sessions?

2. Do you have any areas of particular interest or concern?

3. How can we best measure the effectiveness of these sessions?

4. Can we agree from the start to both be open-minded and frank about how these sessions are going?

5. After each session can we agree on action plans and any other changes as needed?

The last point is particularly important, as it provides an agreed agenda for the next meeting. In that way, both the coach and individual are absolutely clear on the purpose and process of the coaching sessions.

Analyse the Current Situation and Come to an Agreement on the Problems or Issues at Hand

At this stage, the individual explains in detail what is going on and the coach listens and occasionally asks questions. In some cases, this is an opportunity for the individual to let off steam or to talk through a problem they've been struggling with, and the coach is usually advised at first to just let them talk. The coach will then need to ask some probing questions (see "Asking Incisive Questions" below) to be sure the whole picture is being presented and that the dynamics at work are clear. At the end of this stage the coach (and the individual!) should have a clear understanding of what the problems are and together they can move on to the problem-solving stage.

Devise an Action Plan

The next step is to consider all the possible options and the pluses and minuses of each. The coach should facilitate this process but as much as possible should let the individual come up with potential solutions and consider each in detail. For example, if the individual's problems stemmed primarily from time management difficulties, it would be up to them to decide on the possible options available — delegate more, get to work earlier, focus on key tasks, learn to say "no", etc. — and the benefits and risks involved with each. Together, the coach and individual should then be able to decide what course to follow.

Gain a Commitment from the Individual to the Action Plan

This step is crucial. Agreeing to an action plan is one thing and committing to it quite another. At this stage, the coach is pressing the individual to decide *what* they are going to do and *when*. To take the above example, if time management is the problem and the agreed action is to say "no" when overburdened with work, *how* is the "no" going to be delivered and what will the likely responses be? Thinking through the consequences of the plan could be the key to ensuring that it is implemented and successful.

Monitor the Situation and Provide Feedback

In the next and subsequent sessions, it is important to follow up on what was agreed and to discuss its success or otherwise. The coach should be quick to praise positive steps taken by the individual, and if the problem continues show patience but start the process over again. It is up to the individual to make the necessary changes to improve the situation, and the coach's job is to provide the support and encouragement to help them to do so. But ultimately, if the coaching process is to work, the individual must follow through on what they agreed to do. If not, then the coach has every right to express disappointment or even annoyance.

After each coaching session, I ask the individual to write up what we discussed and to send it to me. This ensures that the coach knows how the individual perceived the session and that there is a clear understanding of the issues discussed and any action to be taken. This description of the previous meeting plus the action plan then become the basis for the agenda of the next one.

Length and Location of Coaching Sessions

The key issue regarding length of sessions is that there should be enough time set aside so that the individual never feels rushed. My coaching sessions are normally two-and-a-half hours long, though I always allow for three, just in case additional time is needed. It is also possible to have short coaching sessions, particularly if there is one specific matter to be discussed, though these are less frequent. Different people will have different requirements, however, so the coach should remain as flexible as possible.

The location of the sessions can have an important bearing on how they progress. For example, if the coach is also the individual's direct supervisor, it is almost always a mistake to hold the sessions in the boss's office. The individual is unlikely to feel relaxed and the playing field will hardly seem even. The ideal location is a neutral venue away from the office or, if that is not possible, then in a meeting room. The location needs to be quiet and devoid of any possible interruptions such as telephones ringing or people popping in to ask a question. And whatever you do, avoid carrying out coaching in the home — it simply doesn't work!

Advice for the Coach

Coaching can be exhausting, and the coach should never underestimate the amount of time and energy it requires. It is important to prepare for each session by reviewing notes from previous ones and thinking through how the next session might proceed. It is also advisable to avoid having an important meeting scheduled immediately after a coaching session, partly because you don't want to have time constraints should the session require more time, and also because you need time to reflect on the session, to recover from it and decide on any action you will take before the next session.

The good coach will also make sure that the individual practises self-coaching in between sessions. Coaching is of little value if the individual only focuses on the issues at hand during sessions and then reverts to their usual habits afterwards. They need to be fully aware of the need for self-discipline and self-awareness in order for the coaching relationship to have impact. Indeed, the action plan should include specific examples of how that can be accomplished.

Asking Incisive Questions

To be effective, a coach must develop a clear understanding of the individual and the issues involved. Often the individual is unable or unwilling to express the situation clearly, and it is then up to the coach to devise a way to elicit appropriate and helpful responses. The best method for doing this is to ask specific kinds of questions that require answers that provide an insight into the problem. Below are some examples of the kinds of questions to ask:

- *Open-ended Questions* — These are any questions that require something other than a yes, no or brief response.

  ◊ "Tell me more about your plans to address the issue. . ."

  ◊ "How do you think your boss should be approached . . .?"

  ◊ "What approaches will you take in order to make better use of your time . . .?"

- *Self-discovery Questions* — These questions force the individual to express their own feelings on issues.

  ◊ "How did you feel when you didn't get the rise you expected . . .?"

  ◊ "What did you think her comments about you meant . . .?"

  ◊ "What do you feel has gone well and what have you found to be difficult . . .?"

- *Forward-looking Questions* — These questions require the individual to consider various future scenarios.

◊   "What would you like to be doing in five years' time . . .?"

◊   "If you got that promotion, what would your first steps be . . .?"

- *Overcoming-the-Fear Questions* — These questions help the individual to realise that their fears are unjustified or overstated.

    ◊   "What do you think is the worse that can happen if you speak up in the meeting . . .?"

    ◊   "If the new project doesn't succeed what will your boss do . . .?"

- *Action Questions* — The purpose of these questions is to get the individual to consider taking a specific action.

    ◊   "We've agreed on the issue at hand, what do you intend to do about it . . .?"

    ◊   "To make this project a success, who else has to be recruited . . .?"

- *Support Questions* — These questions force the individual to think of what help is needed to accomplish their goals.

    ◊   "What resources do you need to make your plan a reality . . .?"

    ◊   "What information do you need to solve this problem . . .?"

- *Provocative Questions* — These questions are designed to shock the individual out of their lethargy or complacency.

  ◊ "What will you do if you lose your job . . .?"

  ◊ "What will happen if your team fails to support you . . .?"

  ◊ "What steps will you take today to address this problem . . ?"

- *Accountability Questions* — These questions force the individual to accept accountability for their actions.

  ◊ "Who will be responsible if your team isn't ready for the new project . . .?"

  ◊ "What will you do to ensure your boss has all the information she asked for . . .?"

- *Recap Questions* — These questions would attempt to sum up what has transpired during the coaching sessions.

  ◊ "Now that we are at the end of this process, what would you say is different . . .?"

  ◊ "So what have you learned from these meetings together . . .?"

  ◊ "Of the many points we've discussed, which three do you see as crucial . . .?"

As we have seen, coaching is more of an art than a science, and knowing what kinds of questions to ask to get the desired results is a key attribute of the successful coach. The individual will feel that they have come up with insights on their own, which to a certain extent is true, but the good coach has carefully guided them in the right direction. And, of course, as highlighted before, it is equally important to listen carefully to the answers and make comments which show that you have.

Dealing with Resistance

Every coach will come across individuals who have difficulty responding to certain kinds of questions or discussing certain issues. There may be a variety of reasons for their reluctance, and depending on the importance of the issue, the coach has a variety of possible approaches:

- The coach should acknowledge the resistance as soon as it is evident and try to find the reason behind it through questioning.

- The coach should reinforce the point that the sessions are confidential and check to be sure that there is mutual trust.

- Ask the individual what solution they would recommend to overcome the problem — do not push your own.

- Focus on the initial ground rules and the responsibility of the individual to be open and forthcoming at all times.

- The coach should make it clear that it is not his or her intention to force the individual to do anything they don't want to do — coaching is a collaborative process, not a coercive one.

- If all else fails, the coach should move on to other issues and look for opportunities to come back to the resistance at a later date.

Resistance is a natural and expected response to coaching by some people and the coach should not become disheartened when encountering it. The key is to discover the reason for the resistance — fear of looking foolish, lack of trust, misunderstanding of the nature of coaching, etc. — and then devising the best way to overcome it.

Chapter Four

What Makes a Good Coach?

Just as (almost) everybody would benefit from coaching, it's also true that (almost) everybody could become a good coach if they had the right attitude and developed certain skills. In fact, the aim of this book is to help people do exactly that. On the other hand, some coaches stand out from others due to a combination of skills that are particularly well suited to coaching. Most of these skills — such as communications and problem-solving — are valuable to managers in general, but some are specifically pertinent to coaches — such as building rapport, listening skills and a commitment to others.

In this chapter, we'll look at the particular skills that help to make a good coach, and then cite some of the key mistakes coaches need to avoid in order to be successful.

The Key Skills of Coaching
Building Rapport

If I were to cite one skill that is essential to good coaching, this would be it. Any manager who has difficulty developing rapport with others should avoid coaching altogether. Rapport is at the heart of the coaching process and is an essential component in developing a relationship that will get results.

> ### **Commandment Number Four:**
>
> *Establishing rapport is an absolutely essential coaching skill.*

Rapport is defined in my dictionary as "a close and harmonious relationship in which the people involved understand each other's feelings and ideas". The key words here are "harmonious", which indicates a lack of conflict or stress, and "understand", which suggests that the coach and individual are on the same wavelength. I would add that rapport also includes a strong sense of trust and mutual respect that allows for a free and honest exchange of views.

How does one develop rapport? A good question, and one not easily answered. In some ways, the *desire* to want to develop rapport is a good starting place, since people lacking rapport-building skills generally feel no need for them. Rapport involves *connecting* with the other person and being open to what they are thinking or experiencing. Some tips on building rapport would include:

- Show a genuine interest in the individual's background, hobbies, opinions and so on

- Be sure to be non-judgemental and open — create an equal partnership approach

- Establish some common ground — sports, travel, acquaintances, etc. — that you both share

- Show that the coaching session is topmost in your mind and maintain steady eye contact throughout.

Building rapport is a key interpersonal skill, and while coaches *must* have a certain ability at it, all managers should work at improving their rapport-building skills.

Empathy

Closely connected with rapport-building is the ability to empathise with the individual being coached. Empathy in essence means being able to see things from the other's point of view and to understand their motivations and experiences. Issues concerning empathy can arise in coaching when the two people involved are very different types of people, from very different backgrounds, and so on. For example, a coach who grew up in an ordinary family in a middle class neighbourhood may have difficulty relating to someone who grew up in a mansion and went to an elite public school. The good coach, however, will be able to empathise with the individual's experiences and provide appropriate guidance and support as needed.

A more serious difficulty in terms of empathy for a coach is when they simply do not like the person they are coaching. When the dislike is based on the individual's character flaws, which presumably are hindering their performance (e.g. arrogance, self-centredness, dishonesty, etc.) then it obviously becomes part of the coaching agenda as something that needs to be worked on. In some instances, however, the problem is not so clear-cut and it's just a case of a personality clash. If that should occur – and despite a huge effort, the coach simply can't muster any empathy for the individual – the only answer may be for the sessions to cease and other arrangements to be found.

Listening Skills

In my view, listening skills tend to be undervalued by a lot of people. The reason, perhaps, is that most people think they already know how to listen and therefore give this particular skill little thought. The reality, of course, is that most of us are seriously deficient in this area. While others are talking, our minds are full of the things we want to say, or of the conversation being held next door, or the phone calls we need to make later – anything except what the person opposite us is actually saying.

The business coach cannot afford to fall down in this area. Listening to what people are saying, really hearing how they are responding to a question or comment – even what they are *not* saying – are fundamental to the coaching process. The key is to listen *actively*, not just for the words being said but for the meaning behind them. It requires total concentration and an uncluttered mind — during the coaching session, nothing else should preoccupy the coach except for the conversation itself.

Here are some tips on how to improve listening skills during coaching:

- Eliminate any possible environmental distractions — ensure that there are no interruptions, extraneous noise or other hindrances

- Be sure you are in the proper frame of mind — fatigue, worry about a tight schedule or other work concerns will all detract from listening

- Take notes throughout the session of key points made by the individual to show that you are paying attention

- Check for assumptions or preconceptions — do not assume you know what the speaker will say before they say it

- Monitor body language — remember that non-verbal messages can be as revealing as spoken ones

- Resist making conclusions too soon — hear the entire message before starting to analyse it.

Active listening will lead to understanding, which as we've seen is a prerequisite for successful coaching.

A colleague of mine who is a senior manager was told she gave the impression that she doesn't listen. She felt that it wasn't true, but since perception can be reality, it was something she decided to work on. In her coaching sessions with her team, she started to tape each meeting so that she could play them back and make notes on the important points. She was then able to bring them up in the next session when appropriate, which showed beyond doubt that she had indeed been paying attention.

Communication Skills and Overcoming Resistance

The next essential skill will be a familiar one to managers in today's organisations. Communication skills are an essential component of effective management and should be part of any manager's training and self-development programme.

The importance of communication skills in coaching terms should be self-evident. The coach needs to be adept at identifying the key issues to emerge from a coaching session and then analysing and explaining them in such a way as to ensure the desired response. The coach needs to know what kinds of questions to ask, when to ask them and how to interpret the answers. Add to this the ability to provide constructive and honest feedback and you will achieve sound communication.

When coaching sessions fail, it is often due to the coach's inability to elicit constructive and comprehensive responses to the questions asked. Some individuals can be defensive about, or refuse to admit, their shortcomings, or they may simply be reserved and not forthcoming. The coach needs to understand what the motivation is behind their reticence, and then determine the best strategy to overcome it.

Understanding Human Behaviour

Good coaches are part psychologists. They have either an innate or a trained ability to understand human nature in all its complexity. People are complicated beings, and the coach must determine what makes each individual tick — their self-image, their relationships with others, their true capabilities, their dreams and their fears, and much more.

While formal training in psychology is clearly not essential for coaches, a basic understanding of the various personality types would be extremely useful. As we will see later in this book, different types of people require different approaches in coaching, and familiarity with the characteristics associated with extroverts, introverts, etc. would come in very handy.

Coaches should also be able to interpret body language and other non-verbal clues exhibited by the individual. A person's posture or unconscious habits can say a great deal about their frame of mind. For example, a measured and relaxed response may be contradicted by overly erect posture or a fiercely tapping foot.

Picking up on these signals is important for the coach to get an accurate picture of the individual.

Problem-solving and Negotiation Skills

Problem-solving and negotiation are key skills for managers of all kinds. The complicated nature of most businesses today leads to ample opportunities to practise both. For the coach, however, these skills take on added significance.

Problem-solving is very much at the core of the coaching activity, and the best coaches seem able to bring particular flair and creativity to the process. Because coaching sessions are confidential and conducted in a trusting environment, there is considerable scope for challenging established positions in an attempt to find innovative solutions. The coach must be able to think "out of the box" and be open to a wide range of possibilities.

Negotiation is also at the core of coaching. The coach and the individual will not always see eye-to-eye, yet for coaching to work they need to be in complete agreement about the issues involved and the steps necessary to address them. By its very nature, coaching is a collaborative process, and getting the individual to move in a direction the coach thinks is appropriate requires strong negotiation skills. In many ways, the entire coaching process is based on negotiation, as the coach needs to gently lead the process while ensuring that the individual accepts ultimate responsibility for its success.

Forward-thinking and Proactive

The best coaches resist the urge to dwell on past performance and instead always look ahead. Coaching is about change, and while an understanding of past behaviour can be useful, it is essential that coaching focus its energies on the future. Similarly, coaches and people being coached both need to be proactive rather than reactive. They need to take charge of situations by taking active steps to deal with problems and respond to opportunities.

Flexible Yet Consistent

The next set of skills would at first glance appear contradictory but in reality are complementary. The effective coach needs to maintain a flexible mindset about what works and what doesn't, not only between different individuals but also between different issues and situations for each individual. A coach simply cannot become fixated on one "correct" solution for any particular problem. There are too many variables and people's experiences and requirements are too diverse to be able to follow one consistent course of action.

At the same time, it is important for a coach to be consistent in how they deal with each individual. Coaching is a highly personal process based on trust and the individual must know what they can expect each time they begin a coaching session. Consistency gives the individual a sense of security in the system, and allows them to experiment in a safe environment. Indeed, the process of coaching itself is valuable and a consistent approach by the coach is more likely to lead to success.

Enthusiasm and Commitment to the Individual

The final skills to be discussed here are the less tangible but equally important ones of enthusiasm and commitment to the individual. The importance of enthusiasm should be fairly self-evident, as coaching is about change and development and an unenthusiastic coach is unlikely to encourage either. The best coaches are absolutely sincere in their enthusiasm and honestly hope that the individual will be transformed in a positive way by the coaching process.

The last skill I'm going to discuss, a total commitment to the individual being coached, is indicative of why coaching is such an effective tool in organisations. One of the key benefits to the individual being coached is the fact that they have a champion looking out for their interests. They have someone to go to for advice, for support, for encouragement, for feedback on new ideas and more. The best coaches show great loyalty to the people they coach, and that fact alone explains why coaching can be so powerful.

Coaching Mistakes to Avoid

Just as there are key skills that are essential to becoming a good coach, there are certain mistakes that must be avoided.

Mistake Number 1: Taking on Other People's Responsibilities

Most coaches are successful managers themselves, which means they are used to getting things done. In fact, problem-solving and decision-making are most likely skills they excel at. They are thus likely to feel some impatience at the individual who is not able or willing to think through problems or take the necessary steps to address shortcomings. In many instances, the coach is tempted to "step in" to help move the process along. Clearly this is a mistake, as the collaborative nature of coaching requires the individual to arrive at decisions and to take action themselves. The coach can facilitate the process but the responsibility remains with the individual. This sometimes requires a major shift in thinking for coaches, as they need to become more of a teacher and a guide rather than a decision-maker. Unfortunately, coaches who do take on an individual's problems often find they have become a crutch or source of dependency — and then have a new problem to address.

Mistake Number 2: Too Much Talking, Too Little Listening

Many coaches feel that their business expertise and years of experience mean that they should share what they know with the individual being coached. While this experience is valuable, remember that the coaching process needs to be focused on the individual, not the coach. It is much more preferable for the coach first to sit back and learn as much as possible about the individual and then, if appropriate, provide some guidance through their own experiences. Each individual is unique, but by careful listening and incisive questioning, the coach can understand the issues involved and help the individual to identify solutions that are most appropriate.

Mistake Number 3: Empathising to a Fault

Despite the fact that an ability to empathise is a key skill for coaches, there are times when it can be too much of a good thing. The danger occurs when the coach becomes too soft, placing too much weight on seeing things from the individual's point of view and refraining from challenging issues as much as necessary. Remember that the coaching process needs to look forward, not backward. Acknowledging past difficulties is fine, but the coach's job is to help the individual move forward and make improvements. Sometimes this will involve preventing the individual from self-pity and encouraging them to face up to their problems. Too much empathy can make that task difficult, and not productive.

Mistake Number Four: Coaching for the Wrong Reasons

For some coaches, even some fairly effective ones, the coaching process can become mainly focused on themselves. They may be actually helping the individuals they coach, but they think in terms of what *they* accomplished, how *they* were able to turn the person around, and so on. Some coaches even get a vicarious thrill when their clients achieve a major breakthrough, or go into a major funk if the clients have a particularly bad day. In fact, some coaches identify so strongly with their clients that they are almost trying to relive their lives through them. This can be very dangerous. The coach needs to empathise with the individual, yet keep a certain distance at the same time. The relationship needs to be relaxed and friendly, yet also professional and serious. And the focus should always be on the individual — it should be *their* triumphs, *their* setbacks, and ultimately, *their* decisions.

Mistake Number Five: Unrealistic Expectations

Coaching can accomplish wonderful things, but there are limits. New coaches in particular tend to get carried away by the potential of coaching and expect their clients to accomplish miracles after a few sessions. This, of course, isn't healthy for the coach and isn't fair to the individual. Coaching tends to be an incremental process. There are occasional "breakthroughs", but for the most part it involves a gradual shift in behaviours and attitudes. Coaches must not get impatient when things go slowly or seem to reach a plateau. It is not a "quick fix" answer to an individual's or organisation's problems, but rather a long-term strategy for development. The coach should just acknowledge and celebrate the victories as they occur and keep focused on the goals as agreed in the initial sessions.

Mistake Number Six: Underestimating People's Ability to Change

Notwithstanding the advice above, a common mistake coaches make is expecting too little from their clients. If handled properly, coaching *can* accomplish great things and most people respond to it very well. The old adage that "a leopard never changes its spots" can be proved to be untrue. The coach and individual should set ambitious, but realistic, goals for themselves and decide on the best strategy for achieving them. People need to be stretched to make progress, and assuming that they are incapable of change can quickly become a self-fulfilling prophecy. If the coach does push too hard and the individual objects, they can then discuss the issue and together decide how best to proceed.

Mistake Number Seven: Failing to Coach the Whole Person

We will discuss this in more detail in Chapter Ten, but many coaches make the mistake of focusing solely on the individual's work performance without finding out what else is going on in their lives. In some cases, there is a reticence to pry into personal issues, but to coach effectively one must understand the whole person. For example, if the individual is missing a lot of time at work, there may be personal or family problems involved. Because coaching is a completely confidential activity, the individual should be willing to discuss almost any matter with the coach and together they can consider options. The trend today in employee relations is no longer to separate work lives and personal lives, and the effective coach will need to focus on both. Indeed, there are thousands of examples of managers and directors leading well-balanced lives while performing exceptionally well at work. The coach should strive for similar results with each individual they work with.

Chapter Five

Coaching Styles

There's no one right way to coach. As noted earlier, there are certain fundamentals that should be followed, and there are also certain skills that are useful in order to become a good coach, but different individuals and different situations require different approaches. In this chapter, we look at the various coaching styles that may be adopted, depending on what impact is required.

The idea of switching styles may seem odd to some — especially concerning earlier advice about the importance of consistency! — but I feel it's justified given the wide variety of experiences one is likely to encounter during coaching sessions. Consistency within each style remains important, otherwise the person being coached would have no idea what to expect from one session to the next. But here flexibility is the catchword.

In the next chapter we'll look at the different types of individuals one might come across in coaching — from the underachiever to the high flyer — but in this one we'll focus squarely on the different roles the coach might play in a coaching session. Of course, these styles

are not mutually exclusive and there can be considerable overlap among them. Still, it can be useful to think
in terms of different roles when coaching.

Commandment Number Five:

*There is no one right way to coach —
different people and different situations
require different approaches.*

We'll look at five different coaching scenarios, with
case examples for each:

- The Teacher

- The Listener

- The Supporter or Enabler

- The Parent

- The Taskmaster.

The Teacher

For many, this would be the traditional role one thinks
of for a coach. Here the coach is seen as someone with
expertise and knowledge that they can impart to more
junior or less experienced staff members. In some cases,
the knowledge would be general and the coaching sessions fairly wide-ranging. The individual would pre-

sumably benefit from whatever information the coach could pass on. In other cases, the coach would focus on a specific skill or set of skills. For example, a coach with experience in project management might be chosen to guide a new manager who has just been assigned a major project. Here the coach would concentrate on the specific skills needed to manage a large project.

In the Teacher mode, the coach would play a somewhat more active and direct role than in some others. They would more clearly lead the process and may do more talking than listening, although it would still need to be a clearly collaborative process to work. It would also be somewhat less of a partnership approach than in other styles, as almost by definition the coach has something to "teach" the individual. The relationship, however, should remain as one of equals as much as possible to retain the basic spirit of coaching.

In the Teacher mode of coaching, the sessions would often follow a fairly set pattern. The coach would need to ascertain where the individual currently is in terms of learning and then guide them from the "comfort zone" stage to the "stretch zone" stage. The coach would need to determine what kind of learning style works best for that individual — e.g. Activist, Reflector, Theorist, etc. — and structure the learning accordingly.

The particular skills needed to coach in this style are those involved in any type of learning situation: patience, communication, clarity, etc. The coach should have a good understanding of how learning occurs and by asking appropriate and timely questions check regularly to confirm that learning has taken place. The individual needs to *want* to learn and to be willing to try new things to further their development.

Case Example

One of my clients was asked to coach a fairly capable but very raw young man who had just joined the firm. The young man had graduated from university with a liberal arts degree and though this was his first "real job" he was placed in a fast-track managerial slot, so much was expected of him. In other words, he was considered very promising but there was much to be done. He wasn't familiar with basic accounting and finance principles, knew next to nothing about business strategy, and had only a hazy understanding of human resource management. Fortunately, my client enjoyed a challenge and the young man was particularly bright.

My client decided to embark on a crash course in business management to get the young man up to speed. The coaching sessions were highly structured, with specific readings and assignments, which the young man attacked with relish. In the coaching sessions themselves, my client focused on "real world" business issues that affected the company directly so that the learning was relevant and interesting. After a few months the young man had a functional understanding of the business world and a couple of years later went on to get an MBA. This is an excellent example of the benefits of coaching — in another company it would have taken him years to accomplish what he did in a few months.

The Listener

This coaching style is quite different from the previous one and would cover a variety of situations. As the name would suggest, the focus in this style is primarily on listening and the coach would either act as a sounding board, an adviser or whatever the situation required. In many cases, the coach and the individual would be equals and the approach would clearly be one of partnership.

There are many situations where the Listener style of coaching would be appropriate. Often individuals with specific problems will need a safe place to vent their feelings or to seek help. Confidentiality here is absolutely key, as the individual must feel that they can speak freely without any possible repercussions. For many personal problems (e.g. marital or family problems) there is little the coach can do but lend a sympathetic ear, although if the problems are affecting work performance, a more aggressive response may be called for.

Other coaching situations that could be covered by this style would be the struggling sales manager trying to meet ambitious new targets, the successful manager who is looking for new challenges, or the rising star trying to decide on an appropriate development path. In each case, the effective coach might be the one who lets each individual toss out new strategies, weigh up the pros and cons of a difficult decision, etc. without a great deal of input from the coach. The individuals might just need someone to talk to, and the Listener could be just what the doctor ordered.

Of course, listening skills are not as passive as they seem, and the effective coach will ask probing questions that help the individual greatly in thinking through the issues involved. The coach would challenge the assumptions being made and ensure that the decisions are realistic, reasonable and only arrived at after all aspects of the situation have been considered.

The skills required of the Listener are empathy, a high level of concentration, active listening, incisive questioning and a commitment to the individual.

Case Example

One of the individuals I coached came to me one day with a major dilemma. She had just been offered a very attractive job in her organisation's Australian office. She knew it was a career-making position and desperately wanted to take it, but not surprisingly had many other issues to consider. She was married with two small children who had not yet started school, and her husband had a job that he wasn't wild about, so she thought it might be possible for the family to make the move. Still, she had lived in London all her life, she was close to her parents and brother who lived nearby, and was not anxious to leave. But then the job was a great opportunity. . . . She and I kicked around all the options for about an hour

*— although in reality I probably said about twenty words —
and at the end of the session she still wasn't sure what to do
but felt considerably better. I was then able to ask her some
fairly pointed questions about how she valued her career versus the comforts and stability of her home. The next week we
had another session which covered some of the same ground
but her thinking was becoming more focused. It so happened
that they didn't make the move — but she was able to secure a
promotion almost as good closer to home a year later. In general, this is a good example of the Listener style in action — or
possibly inaction!*

The Supporter or Enabler

The next coaching style would be somewhat of a combination of the Teacher and the Listener. In this style,
the individual has a fairly clear idea of what they want
to accomplish but need help to do so. It would represent a fairly standard view of a task-focused coaching
experience and would probably include the majority of
coaching cases. Examples might include:

- Someone with a fear of public speaking

- An individual looking for help in dealing with a
  boss who is a bully

- A middle-aged manager trying to plan the end of
  his career and ensuing retirement

- Someone under stress due to time management
  problems or an unwillingness to delegate

- A woman who feels that she is not being promoted due to gender reasons.

In each case, the individual knows what they want to achieve and are looking for the coach to provide them with emotional support and practical assistance. In most cases, the individual is unable or unwilling to tackle the problem on their own and the coach is seen as a valuable ally and resource.

The Supporter or Enabler style would cut across most of the other styles in this chapter. Elements of each might be appropriate, depending on the circumstances, but there is a distinction in that there is one clear goal in mind. The coach should be able to focus their energies on that single goal while being aware of related issues that are likely to crop up along the way. As with nearly all coaching sessions, the coach and the individual then need to agree on the goals and objectives, analyse the situation, agree on a strategy, commit to the strategy and then monitor the situation.

The coaching skills required for the Supporter or Enabler would run the gamut of skills mentioned in this book.

Case Example

A colleague of mine coached a young woman named Clare who had a very specific problem. Clare loved her job and was doing very well, but felt that her immediate manager was very patronising towards her. She was in her mid-thirties, and her manager was only ten years or so older, but she felt that he didn't treat her with the same seriousness he did her (mainly male) colleagues. Issues of gender — and age — are increasingly common in organisations today and my colleague was determined to help Clare find a solution to this problem.

The first step was to determine whether Clare's concerns were justified — in other words, was the manager indeed acting in a patronising way. After considerable discussion, my colleague agreed that the complaint was justified and that Clare would need to address the problem. The next step was to ensure that Clare wasn't giving the manager any reason to be patronising, that is, that she was acting professionally at all times. When my colleague was convinced that Clare was in no way at fault, they then considered her alternatives. After much debate they decided that Clare would have to meet with her manager to express her concerns so that the issue would be out in the open. They discussed the pros and cons of this plan and agreed that it was the best course of action. Clare confronted her manager, who denied he had been patronising in any way, but gradually the situation improved.

The Parent

In the Parent style, the coach becomes something of an authority figure and needs to direct the coaching process with a firm hand. In these cases, the individual may be reluctant to accept coaching or somewhat immature in general and strict guidelines need to be set. Here it is clearly more difficult to operate on an equal partnership basis, though, as always, consensus must be reached for the process to work.

In these situations the individual often resists coaching while simultaneously looking for praise and validation from the coach — just as in the typical parent–child relationship. In most cases, however, the coach should be reluctant to adopt the Parent role. It tends to prevent the individual from assuming responsibility themselves, as they look for permission and approval from the coach. It can also lead to dependency by the individual.

On the other hand, the Parent mode can be useful for a brief period in dealing with individuals who have specific needs. Some people need or want to be told what to do and the coach may feel it appropriate to give them guidance to reach specific goals. As noted above, however, eventually the relationship needs to become more equal so that the individual is able to take personal responsibility.

One strategy for overcoming the Parent mode of coaching would be to put the reasons for it at the heart of the coaching session. That is, why does the individual need to seek the approval of others (the coach) before making a decision? Is low self-image or lack of confidence a problem with this person? How can the coach and the individual together attack this problem of dependency? In this way, the coach should eventually be able to leave the Parent mode and move on to one that is more constructive.

Case Example

One of my clients was asked to coach a young woman who had recently joined the company after receiving her MBA. My client enjoyed showing rising managers the ropes and was an excellent teacher. The young woman had done very well in a top business school and arrived at the coaching sessions full of confidence and energy. Unfortunately, she knew a good deal less than she thought she did about how the real world worked and my client had his work cut out for him.

Over several sessions, it became apparent that the young woman's confidence actually veered into arrogance and she was having major difficulty getting along with her non-MBA colleagues. My client decided that he would have to tell her in no uncertain terms why she was having difficulty and what to do about it. He explained that though her skills were strong she would never advance in the organisation if she could not work well with others. Creating a strong team was crucial to success and her attitude was preventing this from happening. The young woman initially took this information very badly, as she had come to look up to my client as a father figure, but eventually began to understand her attitudes and actions better and was able to adjust over time.

The Taskmaster

Not surprisingly, the Taskmaster takes the Teacher several steps further. In this style, the coach needs to be very firm in order to deal with fairly serious problems. The typical case where this style comes into play is with the chronic underachiever who is performing far below their potential. They may have attitude problems or be severely demoralised, possibly even have emotional problems, and it is the coach's task to get to the root of the difficulty and dramatically improve performance.

The Taskmaster tends to be straight-talking and very directive. There is clearly a need to understand what is causing the poor performance, if possible, but there also needs to be a focus on the performance itself. Organisations need to be caring and solicitous towards their employees, but they also need to get high quality work out of them. Coaching can be a godsend in this regard, as the coach can demonstrate concern and a desire to help, but also convey the message that poor performance will not be tolerated indefinitely.

To be effective, however, the Taskmaster still has to keep in mind the fundamentals of coaching, although they can be somewhat more difficult to practise: show sincere interest in the individual and build rapport; ensure confidentiality; focus on learning and changed behaviour; agree on goals; devise a strategy and gain commitment; and monitor the situation and provide feedback. The individual may not always be co-operative, however, which is where negotiation skills come into play.

Unless the fundamentals are followed, the process becomes more like a standard counselling session and the benefits of coaching are lost. But as we have seen with the other styles, the Taskmaster can be extremely effective. The individual is forced to accept that a problem exists and to work with the coach to correct it. Most people, even ones with seemingly poor attitudes, actually want to do good work but are being held back for some reason.

The particular coaching skills associated with the Taskmaster include negotiation, incisive questioning, a commitment to the individual and, above all, perseverance.

Case Example

Early in my managerial career I was asked to coach a young man who was having great difficulty getting along with his colleagues. His work performance in general was adequate, but he had a ferocious temper and had been at the heart of some blazing rows. It had become a very serious problem as some of his colleagues were afraid of him and others felt that his behaviour was bordering on abusive.

As can be imagined, I wasn't looking forward to this particular coaching experience, but plunged ahead nonetheless. I decided to take a two-pronged approach. First I made it clear that his behaviour was inappropriate and would not be tolerated. I wanted him to understand the seriousness of the problem, although I emphasised that together we would work through the issues involved and that a solution would be found. I then started to explore possible causes for his in-credible anger — was it work-related, personal, psychologi-cal, etc. It turned out that he was having very serious problems at home and the stress of the situation simply bub-bled over at work. Together we decided that a course in anger management would be appropriate and found other ways to address the problem as well.

As this and the other examples should illustrate, there are many different approaches a coach can take, de-pending on the nature of the individual and the issues at hand. Some coaches will naturally be more comfort-able with some styles than with others, but it is still use-ful to be aware of the benefits of a flexible approach and a complete focus on the desired end result.

Chapter Six

Coaching the Best . . . and Coaching the Rest

In the last chapter we looked at the different coaching styles that can be used in various situations. In this chapter, we shift the focus to the individuals being coached. Not surprisingly, there are an almost endless number of possibilities here, but to illustrate the effectiveness of coaching, we'll look at six generic types of employees. For each type, we'll look at the kind of issues that would be addressed and how a good coach would go about improving performance. The six types are:

- The High Flyer

- The Underachiever

- The Plodder

- The Talented-but-inexperienced

- The Talented-but-difficult

- The Not-so-talented.

The High Flyer

At first, one would assume that coaching the High Flyer would be fun, and often this is the case, yet there are still many potential issues that can arise. By definition, the High Flyer tends to be committed, enthusiastic and capable, and the unwary coach may be tempted to think that the best option is to just let them get on with it. But there are some problems with High Flyers that I've come across over the years:

- Boredom and restlessness

- Too much ambition, ruthlessness

- Over-confidence

- Unable or unwilling to be a team player

- Impatience with others, attitude of superiority

- Workaholic, lack of balance in life.

In others words, though High Flyers are capable, there can still be much they can learn from coaches. For example, organisations are complicated, relationship-driven entities and High Flyers can have as much or more difficulty getting along with other people as most. The effective coach will be able to spot these shortcomings and address them, while at the same time acknowledging and celebrating their strengths and accomplishments.

If the High Flyer is showing signs of boredom or restlessness, the coach can help them find new challenges or goals. If the problem is one of over-ambition to the point of harming others, the coach will need to work on the High Flyer's empathy and understanding for their colleagues. If being a team player is a weakness, the coach will need to convince the High Flyer that much more can be achieved as a team than they can do on their own. If there are signs of over-confidence and impatience with others, the coach may need to find a way to bring the High Flyer down a peg or two with some straight talking. And if they are working around the clock in order to succeed, the coach will need to stress the importance of balance and perspective as keys to true success.

As we will see throughout the book, coaching is for (almost) everyone and even the High Flyer is likely to have many things to work on. The trick for the coach is to first discover exactly what they are, and then to devise effective strategies for dealing with them.

Fortunately, most High Flyers take well to coaching, as they are bright, ambitious and willing to listen to good advice. They tend to enjoy the collaborative process of coaching and want to be active participants in their own business and personal growth. They also tend to be quick on the uptake and, once they are convinced of the correct course of action, are usually able to make rapid improvements.

Case Example

One of the companies that I work with asked me to coach a young woman who had considerable potential. There wasn't an opening there at the moment for advancement and they were concerned that she would go elsewhere if they didn't offer her some way to further her development.

In our first session, we discussed the overall programme for her that had been agreed with the Human Resources Director, which included two outside courses, a three-month secondment to a major project, and regular one-to-one coaching sessions with myself. I explained that the organisation had great confidence in her and high expectations, which meant that in our sessions I was going to challenge her to be performing at a high standard at all times.

In jointly looking for areas of improvement, we agreed that she could at times be too impatient, even when tackling important issues. This gave the impression that she was somewhat superficial and couldn't be trusted when it mattered. We agreed that this could be a barrier to advancement and discussed what might be done about it. She finally admitted that she would need to work harder on her preparation and follow-up, especially on the priority issues. Over time, this High Flyer improved her performance considerably and went on to higher levels in all aspects.

The Underachiever

As a rule, people in this category tend to cause coaches a good deal of frustration — though equally it can end with a considerable amount of satisfaction. As the name implies, Underachievers are not living up to their potential for some reason and the coach needs to ascertain why and what to do about it. Here again, the value of the coaching process over other forms of intervention — training, counselling, performance appraisal, etc — is apparent, as often only the coach has the time and expertise to work through the issues involved.

In order to work successfully with the Underachiever, it is essential to get to the root cause of the problem. This will clearly vary from individual to individual, but some causes might include:

- Fear of failure

- Lack of confidence

- Laziness, lack of ambition

- Personal problems

- Poor attitude, chip on the shoulder

- Lack of training or education

- Interpersonal or communication difficulties.

In each instance, the coach first needs to get a clear picture of what's going on, and then devise a programme with the individual to address it. For example, if the problem is a fear of failure, the coach needs to work on building up the individual's confidence and help them to gradually take a few risks. If poor attitude is the problem, the coach will force the Underachiever to face up to the reality of their poor attitude and try to ascertain its source. If the individual is simply not adequately trained for their position, the coach will help them to get whatever assistance is needed.

As with all coaching situations, the individual must be prepared and willing to make changes. This can obviously be a problem with the Underachiever, and there will be times when there is nothing the coach can do if there is not a sincere desire for improvement. For individuals showing reluctance to change, the coach should aim for gradual incremental improvements that can be celebrated and discussed. Here the coach needs to show patience and not expect miracles. On the other hand, a sudden breakthrough with an Underachiever can more than make up for the time spent.

Different Underachievers will respond to different approaches, but often the Parent or Taskmaster styles discussed in the previous chapter will get the best results. The Underachiever typically needs to be prodded and cajoled into action, which requires a somewhat stricter approach than some other coaching styles.

Case Example

I once coached a young man who had done very well at university and was highly thought of by his colleagues, but who seemed to lack ambition. He had reached somewhat of a plateau in his career and seemed quite happy just to remain where he was, though I suspected that he was capable of much more. I decided to challenge him on his lack of ambi-

tion, as I was frustrated at his sense of complacency. At first, he denied that there was anything wrong and insisted that he was quite content with his lot. As I probed a bit further, however, I realised that this capable young man had a horrible fear of failure. He had convinced himself that he wouldn't be able for more serious responsibility and was afraid that he wouldn't know what he was doing and would look foolish. We discussed his concerns in more detail and then agreed that they were something we would work on in further sessions. Over time, he was able to take more risks without disaster striking and his confidence gradually increased to the point that his fear of failure disappeared completely. Not surprisingly, his value to the organisation also grew.

The Plodder

For most coaches, this category of individual would be their least favourite. The Plodder is the type who just gets through the workday without much enthusiasm or imagination, but without causing any real problems either. They often simply don't have much ambition, though in some rare cases they have hidden abilities and talents that the exceptional coach can identify and bring to the surface.

Usually, however, the Plodder has found their right level in the organisation and is relatively content with it. Unlike the Underachiever, the coach rarely gets the sense that they have untapped potential and thus the coaching sessions can be a good deal less interesting. In fact, the Plodder would rarely volunteer to be coached

at all, and in most cases attend coaching sessions because everyone on their team is doing so or they are
being coerced into it for some other reason. This lack of
enthusiasm for the process, and general unwillingness
to change, tends to doom the coaching effort to failure.

If the coach becomes truly convinced that they are
dealing with a Plodder, their options are somewhat
limited. Usually they will attempt to find one area or
aspect of the job that the individual enjoys or shows
enthusiasm for and try to develop it further. In some
cases, they might try to challenge them into stretching
themselves somewhat, but the true Plodder will usually
disappoint. The coach with considerable patience will
keep trying to find areas to work on, but for most there
will come the realisation that this is one of the 10 per
cent or so that simply cannot be coached. The true
Plodder will be relieved to return to the routine of their
job and will rarely take offence if the coach suggests
that the coaching sessions are a waste of time.

In their attempt to get through to the Plodder, the
coach may try each of the coaching styles described
earlier, alternating between the Listener, the Parent, the
Taskmaster, and so on. If each style results in failure,
however, the coach may need to adopt one final new
style: the Realist!

Case Example

*"George, you're good for the organisation because you can
always be relied upon to do a satisfactory job," was how one*

coach began his session. The coach knew that George was typical of a nucleus of people in one particular department who did adequate work — no more and no less. There were no real complaints about George's work performance, but not much praise either.

During the sessions, the coach tried very hard to discover what made George tick, to discover any hidden talents that could be brought to the surface. The coach himself was a dynamic and ambitious man who had great difficulty understanding how someone could just float through life seemingly without goals or challenges. After several sessions, the coach had made little headway, however, as George really seemed quite content with his lot.

The coach decided that the best approach was to accept George's limitations but to be sure that he still felt that he was a valued member of the team. There was little point in trying to transform George into something he either could not or would not become, but there was equally no reason for overlooking the contribution he did make. The coaching sessions actually went very well, as George was able to express his views on the strengths and weaknesses of the team and left the sessions feeling very much appreciated.

The Talented-but-inexperienced

The coaching process for this category is not complicated. This type of individual has definite potential but typically needs either more work experience or more formal training. The goal for the coach is to identify the areas where experience is needed and then determine the best strategy for acquiring it. The coach will often take a task-based approach, whereby the individual is expected to learn very specific skills.

The coach will often assume the Teacher mode described earlier to either impart information directly or to identify sources where it can be found. For example, someone who has been promoted to their first managerial position may need some basic training in the fundamentals of management. This may involve taking outside courses, reading books on management, watching management videos, etc. The coach is there to guide the process, offer advice, answer any questions or help to deal with difficult situations, or even just provide encouragement and general support. Here again, coaching is by far the best method for bringing inexperienced employees up to speed.

Talented-but-inexperienced people are almost always very receptive to coaching and difficulties seldom occur. As with all coaching sessions, the goal should be to keep their confidence and enthusiasm levels high, while helping them to learn new things and to grow in the job. The coach will often see fairly rapid improvement and needs to ensure that the individual is being adequately challenged and stretched at all times.

Case Example

I was once asked to coach a young man who had just been promoted to his first managerial position. He was a college graduate and very bright but had very little experience in the

business world. Our first task was to focus on the require-
ments of the job itself, to be sure he understood how each
could best be carried out. We then moved on to broader issues
that would determine how he performed overall, such as time
management, communication skills, prioritisation, and so on.
Over time we were able to isolate specific areas that could use
improvement, which helped his development considerably.

The Talented-but-difficult

Any category with the word "difficult" in it will obviously present a challenge to the coach. This group includes people who have the potential to become High
Flyers if only they could get along with those above,
below and next to them. Unfortunately, they don't, and
it's up to the coach to find a strategy that will lead to
some improvement.

Often, the first step is to create self-awareness. People in this category seldom think of themselves as difficult and would say that they are "fighting their own
corner", or "not willing to be walked on" or "sticking to
their guns" or some other phrase for defending their
behaviour. The coach will try to get them to see things
from the point of view of others to realise the impact of
their behaviour. In other words, the coach will try to
create empathy in someone who is too self-centred or
defensive to see how their actions are perceived.

The coaching style to use here would be that of the
Parent, as often the individual is acting like a child who
simply wants their own way. The coach needs to ex-

plain the benefits and necessity of teamwork and emphasise to the individual that the ability to get along
with others is quite fundamental to success of any kind.
An effective approach is to ask a series of challenging
questions aimed at helping the individual to understand for themselves where mistakes are being made in
their relationships with others, and the negative impact
this has on the team.

It is important, of course, when dealing with the Talented-but-difficult not to ignore the "talented" part of
the equation. That is, while working on the person's
interpersonal shortcomings, one should still acknowledge their strengths and achievements as well. In that
way, their overall confidence won't be damaged and
the message is much more likely to be received and
acted upon.

Case Example

*I once had a client who was bright, enthusiastic and had a
reputation for getting things done. In other words, exactly
the kind of person organisations are looking for these days.
Unfortunately, she was also very impatient with others and
tended to make a lot of people angry and uncomfortable with
her attitude.*

*Knowing that she had real potential, I decided to first try
to get her to admit that her intolerance was a problem so that
we could tackle it together. I said to her, "I'm told that you
are someone who is able to get things done, yet you have a
reputation for not suffering fools gladly and in fact can be*

quite insensitive. Why do you think that is?" After some dis-cussion of the issue, I then suggested that her impatience with others was a kind of self-indulgence and asked her what she thought the long-term impact on her performance would be if it continued. She eventually agreed that it was a serious problem and together we were able to devise a plan of action that would improve her people management skills. It worked very well and her relationships with others gradually im-proved considerably.

The Not-so-talented

The final category I'm going to discuss is another one that presents difficulties for the coach. This group in-cludes people who for whatever reason do not have what it takes to succeed in their current position in the organisation. In some cases they may have been pro-moted to a level beyond their capabilities, or in other cases they may simply be in the wrong job or have been in it too long. Some may have a very good attitude but lack the necessary skills, while others may realise they are out of their depth and are miserable. Whatever the case, the coach will be thoroughly challenged to handle it well.

Here are some typical examples of the Not-so-talented at work:

- The salesman who is not good with people

- The manager who is disorganised and cannot pri-oritise

- The public relations person who can't communicate

- The accountant who is sloppy and careless

- The team leader who does not have the respect of
  the team.

In each of these cases, the coach will make every effort
to correct the situation by focusing on the areas of
underperformance or concern and devising strategies
to improve them. Sometimes, however, the problem is
beyond the capabilities of the coach and individual together to solve and alternatives need to be addressed.
One of the fundamentals of effective coaching is that
the coach be honest in their assessment of the situation
and to deal with the reality of it. If, after every effort,
the salesman still can't sell or the accountant is still
careless, it does little good to pretend otherwise.

As with most other coaching situations, however,
the key is for the coach to use their best judgement in
assessing the individual. It would be clearly unfair to
give up on someone too early, and a good coach would
spend a great deal of time with the individual to determine, and indeed often re-establish, their true capabilities and desires. In many cases, the individual has
been sent to a coach as part of a performance assessment or disciplinary process and will be well aware
that the situation has become serious. Some will rise to
the occasion and make a major effort at improvement;

others will not and will need to discuss appropriate alternatives.

The experienced coach will be honest with the Not-so-talented, but supportive and encouraging at the same time. In many cases, the individual will be unhappy at the current situation and welcome the chance to make a change, and the coach must help them retain their self-esteem and approach the matter with a positive attitude.

Case Example

Barry worked for a blue chip company and had built a comfortable niche for himself as a sub-manager to the Finance Director. He was content with his situation until suddenly the business became much tougher and a new Finance Director was hired. It soon became apparent that Barry's work was actually not up to scratch and he had become nothing more than a passenger. It was clear something would have to be done.

The new Finance Director decided to carry out a series of coaching sessions to try to improve the situation. It soon became clear that Barry had become somewhat stale in the job and had basically lost interest. They discussed the problem at length and it was agreed that Barry's new boss would start to challenge him more to see how he would respond. He made it clear that the company needed higher quality work out of Barry but that they were willing to work with him to achieve it. Unfortunately, this was one of those situations where Barry was simply not up to the task. After quite a few ses-

sions, Barry and the Finance Director agreed that the situation could not continue and Barry eventually left the company.

Chapter Seven

Coaching Downwards, Upwards and Sideways in the Organisation

Up to this point we have discussed coaching in fairly general terms. In this chapter we will look at coaching specifically in the context of the organisation. As we will see, the coaching process can take on a very different meaning depending on the relationships between the coach and the individual being coached. For example, coaching one's immediate superior involves some obvious dangers!

We will look at three possible coaching situations in the organisation and assess the opportunities and challenges for each:

- *Coaching downwards*, meaning coaching individuals who report directly to the coach;

- *Coaching upwards*, meaning the relatively unusual situation of coaching one's superior; and

- *Coaching sideways*, meaning coaching one's colleagues or equals in the organisation.

Coaching Downwards

Coaching downwards would be the most typical coaching situation, yet it nevertheless presents its own challenges and dangers. As we have seen, the key to successful coaching is the rapport between the coach and the individual and the honesty of views being expressed. When the coach is the individual's direct manager, however — in other words, responsible for their salary, promotion possibilities, performance evaluation, workload, etc. — it is more difficult for an honest exchange to take place. Since coaching is a collaborative process, the coach and the individual should meet on an even playing field. This is something the coach needs to be continually aware of.

For example, if the individual is frustrated by the work they are being given or their failure to be promoted, the coach is most likely to be the very cause of their frustration. In many ways, this presents an ideal opportunity to deal with the problem, but it does take courage and trust for the individual to freely express their views on the issue. Most people, I feel, would be hesitant to say what they really think to their supervisor, which makes the coaching job much more difficult.

One obvious danger in coaching downwards is for the sessions to resemble standard performance appraisal or counselling meetings. To do so would negate the benefits of coaching and must be avoided at all costs. Performance appraisal is more of a top-down approach and coaching must be collaborative to be effective.

The onus here is on the coach to set the proper tone and ground rules for the coaching sessions. To develop rapport, the coach may need to put aside, to a certain extent, the explicit reporting relationship and treat the individual as an equal. For coaching to be effective, the individual *must* feel that they can express views freely without fear of reprisal or repercussions of any kind. This can be difficult for the coach if the views include explicit or implied criticism of them, although on the other hand it is very healthy to get such views out in the open where they can be dealt with. The coaching process depends on this kind of honesty, and indeed is one of the reasons why it is superior to alternative types of relationships.

For the coach, coaching downwards has numerous benefits. They get a much clearer and more complete picture of each staff member and can develop a close working relationship with each. They also develop a strong sense of the strengths and weaknesses of each person, as well as their potential and attitude. In addition, they are able to assess how people are working together as a team and to deal with any developing problems before they reach crisis stage. A good coach will create a strong sense of loyalty in their staff and get much higher quality work out of each person.

The benefits for the individual are equally apparent. Assuming that a sense of trust and honesty has been established, the individual will understand exactly how they are viewed by their supervisor and where improvements can be made. They also have an opportunity to express any dissatisfaction with how they or the team are being treated and to take an active part in the group. In general, they feel like they can make a valued contribution to their workplace.

In general, coaching downwards has tremendous potential but only if the coaching fundamentals are followed. Rapport must be established, a safe and open environment must exist, and the process must be approached in an honest and collaborative way by both parties.

Coaching Upwards

While this would not be the most typical occurrence of coaching, there are clear benefits — and a few dangers — to coaching upwards. In nearly all cases, coaching upwards only happens at the request of the more senior person, as it might seem a bit impertinent for a junior person to suggest coaching their superior! Still, many senior managers who are secure and confident in their abilities welcome feedback from all sources, including those reporting to them.

Commandment Number Six:

Coaching can also be very effective upwards and sideways in the organisation.

There has also been a significant change in recent years in how managers and directors are developed. Increasingly, senior executives are seeking the views of those who report to them to get a better understanding of how they're doing as managers or leaders. For example, many organisations have introduced the 360° appraisal system, whereby each individual asks a variety of people to rate their performance in key areas. Other organisations have introduced formal upward appraisal programmes on the theory that the only way to gauge the effectiveness of a leader is to ask the people they lead. It is clearly only a small step to move from upward appraisal to actually coaching upwards.

The typical upward coaching session results from a manager wanting to get a clearer sense of their leadership or managerial capabilities from a staff member. It is unusual in coaching terms, as in this case the person being coached tends to lead the process and the "coach" is responding to their questions. To be effective, however, the coaching fundamentals once again have to be followed for an honest and collaborative exchange to take place. It should also be an ongoing process, though as discussed below, this can present problems and is somewhat unusual.

The dangers, of course, are many. The more junior "coach" may have doubts that their superior actually wants an honest view, and there are certainly times when that is the case. An insecure manager may be looking for validation and confirmation from their team and react badly to a sincere expression of their shortcomings. The unfortunate "coach" then has to worry about possible repercussions.

Even when the senior manager is looking for an honest view of their performance, the more junior coach may be reluctant to give it to them. It simply goes against the grain in many organisations to give honest criticism of one's superiors and to work successfully, the rapport and ground rules must be very clearly established.

As we saw above, any time there is explicit inequality between the coach and individual, the coaching process is more difficult. Since the coach typically is expected to guide the sessions, ask penetrating questions, challenge assumptions, and so on, it takes a strong individual to be able to perform that role with a superior. There can also be issues of confidentiality, whereby a senior manager is reluctant to express views about their colleagues or the organisation, or indeed themselves, to a more junior person. Again, to succeed a sense of trust is paramount.

Another danger would be how coaching upwards is viewed by others in the organisation. Colleagues of the more junior "coach" may wonder why he or she has been selected to coach their superior. Suspicion and resentment can easily follow. For this reason, coaching upwards is more likely to be a one-off session, or two at most, as otherwise the balance in the organisation can be adversely affected.

I recently came across an excellent example of coaching upwards in a large company that was upgrading their information technology system. Many of the more senior managers had failed to stay abreast of the new technologies and there was a serious concern that it was affecting their productivity. The company found a very creative solution, however. They decided to have the younger, more junior managers, who were very comfortable with the new technologies, coach their superiors to bring them up to speed. The senior managers accepted the wisdom of this with good grace, and the junior managers were delighted to be able to influence and add value to the upper echelons.

Coaching Sideways

Coaching sideways has many of the benefits and few of the dangers of the previous two possibilities. By its very nature, it tends to involve equals, which can encourage a collaborative approach. There are also few reasons not to be completely honest in the views expressed, as there is less likelihood of negative repercussions.

Nevertheless, for coaching sideways to work, the relationship between coach and individual being coached must be made clear. That is, why does one perform one role and the other a different one? It may be that, although the two have equal status on the organisational chart, one might have more experience in general or specific expertise in a certain area. In that case, the coaching relationship would be clear.

A distinction, of course, needs to be made between formal coaching and two colleagues having a chat about a problem. For it to be actually *coaching*, the process itself must be acknowledged by both the coach and the individual, and the goals and ground rules need to be discussed and agreed. All the other fundamentals of coaching must also be observed for it to work.

Coaching sideways can be particularly effective when the coach and individual are in different parts of the organisation — that is, not working in the same team or for the same boss. If they are too close, then there is a danger of rivalry creeping in, as well as issues around confidentiality. If they were in different sections, however, they would be able to discuss similar issues without directly affecting the other. They would also then gain an insight into how other parts of the organisation operate, how other senior managers relate to staff, what works and what doesn't and so on.

The benefits for both the coach and individual being coached in this case should be evident, but there are also benefits for the organisation. The exchange of views between people in different parts of the organisation helps to increase the knowledge of both and to create a healthy company culture in general.

Indeed, as more and more organisations emphasise the benefits of coaching at all levels, these benefits become increasingly apparent. As noted earlier, coaching-based organisations tend to have a strong company culture with similar values running throughout it. Also, since the best coaches are coached themselves, companies that practise coaching downwards, upwards and sideways in the organisation enjoy its benefits at all levels.

Chapter Eight

Coaching in Times of Turbulence

The benefits of coaching are apparent in a variety of situations, but none more so than when there is a great deal of turbulence brought about by disruptive change — which these days seems to be most of the time. When times are difficult, a coach can help an individual determine exactly what is happening, decide how to deal with the problem, keep matters in perspective, stay focused and optimistic, and much more. Indeed, the coach can be an adviser, confidante, supporter or friend, as needed.

In this chapter we'll look at two types of turbulence:

- *Organisational turbulence*, which can include, for example, downsizing, restructuring, change of ownership, sweeping changes in IT systems, new competitive pressures, and so on; and

- *Personal turbulence*, which can include a new job, changes in responsibility, a new boss, family issues, health problems, stress-related pressures, etc.

As we will see, for both kinds of turbulence coaching can be extremely useful, which leads me to my Commandment Number Seven:

> ### Commandment Number Seven:
>
> *In times of personal or organisational turbulence, coaching can be an absolute godsend.*

The Coach as Change Agent

One of the key benefits of coaching is that it is a particularly effective way to deal with issues of change for an individual or organisation. For anyone facing a major transition of any kind, coaching can help to focus on the issues involved, decide on the options available, address any uncertainty or insecurity associated with the change, and devise an appropriate action plan. The coach's role becomes that of the change agent, someone who can help the individual to accept the reality of the change and formulate the best response. This is particularly true when the change is especially severe or even traumatic.

Since change has become the norm for most organisations and individuals these days, it is imperative that strategies be found for dealing with it. The great advantage of coaching is that it can help to understand the nature of the change in the first place, work through its implications and challenges, and then to identify the most appropriate response.

Organisational Turbulence

One spends a great deal of time in the workplace and when major a change occurs, it can be extremely disruptive. As we saw in the opening chapter, the nature of work has changed considerably in recent years, and for the most part the change has meant greater insecurity and uncertainty for employees at all levels in the organisation.

Downsizing

The trend in recent years of downsizing organisations may have slowed somewhat, but there are still many people suffering from its consequences. In general, it has meant *fewer employees*, which increases the workload and responsibility on others; *more pressure*, since more is now expected of fewer people; *more insecurity* (who will be the next to go?); and *more stress*, for all of the above and other reasons. For coaches, downsizing represents a major challenge for those individuals affected by its consequences.

The coach's response could be twofold: first, to lend a supportive ear and let the person express their worry and frustration; and, second, to help the person view the change in a more positive light. For example, those who survive a major downsizing must be valued em-

ployees with a bright future in the organisation. Rather
than bemoan the loss of help and added work, the individual should see it as a challenge and an opportunity to make an important contribution. If, however,
the stress becomes unbearable, the coach should help
the individual devise a strategy for approaching their
boss to find a solution to the problem.

Change of Ownership

Any time a company acquires new owners, some uncertainty is inevitable. Employees will wonder what the
new owners will do differently from the old, where
they fit in to the new scheme of things, how the company culture or ethos is likely to change, how to per-
sonally respond to that change, and so on. The coach in
these situations will try to assuage any unrealistic fears
and shift the focus to possible positive impacts. The
coach will also help any affected individuals take steps
to benefit from the changes in a proactive manner,
rather than waiting to react when it might be too late.

New Competitive Pressures

Many organisations are experiencing increased competition due to globalisation and a host of other factors.
This can lead to a variety of problems for individuals
involved, such as increased workload, strained relations with superiors, missed sales targets, and so on.
The coach will need to address each of these issues in-
dependently to find possible solutions. The increase in

competition is unlikely to disappear, so individuals and their coaches need to accept this new reality and devise strategies to deal with it.

Rapid and Continuous Change

Organisations — and the individuals inside them —no longer have the luxury of finding a winning formula and then settling into a comfortable and predictable routine as the profits roll in. Today, change is perpetual and organisations and individuals need to constantly seek new skills and improved processes to survive. By its very nature, change is unsettling and the coach can be very helpful in getting people to understand it and respond to it. Often this requires a new way of thinking or possibly developing expertise in a new area and the coach can be instrumental in making the right choices.

One individual who I coach once a quarter requests that we focus three years ahead on how all aspects of her business may change (she feels that longer than that is impossible) and on how she might respond to it. She then uses the outcome of our sessions in the coaching of her own staff to get them to try to see the big picture and keep abreast of change.

New Technologies and New Work Practices

Aligned with the issue of continuous change is the fact that the way people work and the technologies they use are being transformed regularly. A few years ago, no one had even heard of e-mail and today it is funda-

mental to the way we do business. These new technologies and new work practices require continual
learning, which puts added pressure on individuals.
Again, coaches can be very helpful in sorting through
the issues involved and coming up with possible responses.

An example of this is that more and more management information is being provided at an increasingly
faster rate. Decision-making therefore has to reflect this,
which adds to the pressures at all levels. The coaching
sessions are often used to help individuals understand
and focus on the real priorities — priorities that can
change from day to day. Coaches thus have to work on
flexibility, agile and creative thinking, rapid but high
quality decision-making, and so on.

Personal Turbulence

An even greater source of subject material for coaching
sessions stems from issues relating to turbulence in
one's personal life. There are a wide variety of topics
here, both in the workplace and at home, but we will
look at just six fairly common ones.

New Job, New Responsibilities

Whenever someone is promoted to a new position,
certain anxieties are likely to arise. Concerns about
measuring up to expectations, getting along with the
new boss, dealing with the new staff and so on are
common enough. If things then go wrong, these con-

cerns multiply many times over and help is then needed. The coach can help to alleviate these concerns by firstly explaining that they are normal enough and that they should be expected and, secondly, by helping the individual analyse each problem and look for solutions. If getting along with the new staff is a problem, then the coach will help to isolate where the conflict occurs and suggest appropriate responses. If the workload is too great, the coach will look at time management and productivity solutions, or possibly recommend a frank discussion with the individual's new boss. Whatever the issue, the coach can help the individual understand the source of the problem and identify possible solutions.

New Boss

Similar to the above, getting a new boss is another common source of unease for many people. Typically, a comfortable working relationship had been formed with the old boss and there is a natural reluctance to go through the process again. Of course, there is no alternative and the good coach will simply try to alleviate any irrational fears and focus on how the individual can develop a positive relationship with the new one.

One client I had came to me in a very anxious state, worried about the new boss she was getting. She had heard through the grapevine that he was an absolute tyrant and was very sorry that her current boss — who everyone agreed was very easy to get along with, if a bit disorganised — had been transferred to another division. I was able to calm her down and told her to wait and see how things turned out. If there were indeed serious problems, we would work them out together. A month later, she came back all smiles and said that her new boss was great — straight talking, serious but fair, very efficient and results-oriented. She realised that she would have to get used to his different style, but was confident that she could make the adjustment.

Family Issues

Problems outside the workplace can often be more difficult for the coach than ones inside it. The coach has to walk a fine line between helping the individual deal with the problem and prying into their personal life. The general rule would be that if the problem is impacting on job performance, it needs to be discussed, but the coach does need to be aware of the individual's right to privacy.

Family problems that can crop up would include marital difficulties, problems with wayward children, responsibilities for ageing parents, and so on. In most cases, the coach needs to show concern and provide whatever assistance possible, while retaining a focus on the individual's responsibilities at work. For particularly serious problems, there may be a possibility of time off from work or flexible hours, though much would depend on the specifics of individual cases. Often, just having someone who cares to talk to can be an enormous help.

Health Problems

Similar to the above, the nature of the health problems and the overall circumstances will determine the coach's response. Assuming the problem is not work-related (i.e. an injury or an illness which is directly related to the person's job), the coach will need to focus on the nature of the problem and how it affects job performance. Most organisations have company policies which outline the options available to employees with health problems, and the coach can help the individual work through these to decide on the best approach. Again, the coach can provide whatever support and assistance is appropriate.

Stress

This is a particular type of health problem that is occurring more and more often in today's organisations. Typically, this problem would be work-related and the coach can often be instrumental in devising a useful response. The coach will first try to identify the precise causes of the stress and then look for possible ways to alleviate it. For example, if the stress is due to overwork, the coach may focus on time management strategies to reduce the workload. If it stems from interpersonal problems — difficulty getting along with a colleague, feeling of being bullied by the boss, sexual

harassment, etc. — the coach will try to get an understanding of the seriousness and validity of the complaint and then come up with an appropriate plan to
deal with it.

Stress can be extremely debilitating and may lead to
serious health problems. The coach will therefore need
to be alert to its symptoms and provide whatever assistance is available to improve the situation.

Substance Abuse Problems

If an individual confides to the coach that they are suffering from substance abuse problems, the coach will
typically have several fairly clear-cut options available.
Most organisations have policies in place to deal with
such problems and the coach would need to adhere to
them. The coach can then explain to the individual the
seriousness of the problem, the options and support
available and together they can decide what to do.

Often, however, the individual does not admit to
having a problem, although the coach might suspect
that they do. Here the coach clearly needs to be careful.
Their role is to provide assistance and support to people, not to police them. If the behaviour strongly indicates that there is a problem — tardiness or missed
days of work, lack of concentration, irrational behaviour and so on — the coach may challenge the individual to admit to it. But if the challenge is met with strong
denials, there is little to coach can do besides focusing
on the inappropriate behaviour and look for other ex-

planations. If the coach is truly convinced that there is a problem, the individual continues to deny it, and the sessions become non-productive, the coaching relationship should most likely be terminated.

Unlike any other form of one-to-one intervention, coaching is ideally suited to dealing with problems stemming from disruptive change, whether its origin is organisational or personal. Instead of the individual trying to cope with the chaos on their own, the coach provides a supportive ear that can help to overcome difficulties and find possible solutions. As more and more individuals and organisations are buffeted by the winds of change, coaching provides an essential means of keeping one's feet firmly on the ground.

Chapter Nine

The Mentor-Coach:
Creating Effective Leaders

This chapter is somewhat close to my heart as it represents the bulk of my activity these days. I have been fortunate to work as a mentor-coach to some of the top business people in the UK and have learned a great deal from each one of them. Though related to other forms of coaching, the process is a little different when working with senior executives. As we will see, however, many of the same fundamental principles apply.

My dictionary defines *mentor* as "a wise or trusted adviser or guide", which would certainly be how we would like to be perceived. Because we are working with senior executives who have achieved a certain status, it would not be strictly accurate to call the process *coaching*. Yet senior executives have their own personal and business goals to work on, which would not be that dissimilar from those of other individuals being coached. To solve this definitional dilemma, I have therefore settled on the term *mentor-coach*, which in effect covers all possibilities!

Acting as a mentor-coach can be thoroughly satisfying, as the executives tend to be thoughtful, accomplished, sincere and articulate. I am frequently
impressed by the high calibre of people I'm privileged
to work with and their fervent desire to continually
work on their own development.

That is not to say, of course, that the sessions themselves are always straightforward or without difficulties.
Many senior managers are under considerable strain to
produce at a high level, and being human, this can lead
to a whole slew of personal and professional problems.

One of the biggest differences in dealing with senior
executives is that they typically carry around an enormous weight of responsibility. They often have a great
number of people relying on them, looking to them for
guidance or support and some greatly feel the strain.

The Need for Leaders

Much has been written in recent years about the short-
age of real leaders in organisations today. This is in
spite of the fact that there is an increasing awareness of
the importance of the need for more leaders and for
managers to make the transition to leadership. Why is
this so? My belief is that senior executives simply do
not have the time to lead their people, and are never
taught or encouraged to do so. Again, coaching could
be a very useful tool in this regard.

A mentor-coach can help a senior executive understand better the difference between being a leader and

being a manager. A leader will be aware that they have to do far more than what's on their job description — they need to add real value to the organisation and get the best work possible out of their people. They need to have the right mental attitude that enables them to take risks, to be tolerant of mistakes, to lead by example and to be optimistic and forward-looking.

Working with Senior Executives

For the coach, working with senior executives can present a serious challenge. They are typically accomplished and confident people who may not feel that you, the coach, have much to offer them. They also seldom have their views questioned and are used to getting their own way. The coach needs to develop rapport and understanding, but also must be able to "read between the lines" to get a true picture of the individual. In addition, the mentor-coach must have the courage of their convictions and be willing to tell the individual exactly what they think. Being a mentor-coach is definitely more an art than a science, and one that is typically only learned through experience over time.

Below are some of the issues that arise in coaching sessions with senior executives:

- *Leader as Role Model*. The manager who has risen to a senior level in the organisation must be aware that they have a new responsibility and will be watched carefully by those above and below them. Often they will be unaware of the impact their words or actions have on others and the coach needs to make this clear to them.

- *Integrity and Ethics.* Aligned to the above is the need for the leader to act in an ethical way at all times. It is of little use to preach in one way and behave in another, and the leader has a particular responsibility to represent the values of the organisation. The coach can help to keep this ethical approach in the leader's mind at all times, and to challenge them whenever it goes astray.

- *Solving Problems.* Leaders are people who make problems manageable for those below them. The coach can help them consider all the options and find the right approach.

- *Building Trust.* Trust is increasingly important in organisations today as employees take on more responsibility and have less direct supervision. The leader needs to create an atmosphere where trust can flourish, which means allowing risks to be taken and mistakes to be made. The coach can help sort through the issues involved.

- *Creating Loyalty.* Where trust is established, loyalty tends to follow. The leader who earns the loyalty of their team can accomplish great things. If the loyalty is not there — call in the coach.

- *Providing Direction and "Vision"*. The leader is expected to know where the organisation is headed and how it should get there. If a leader isn't sure about either, the coach can help to work through the issues involved.

- *Inspiring the Team*. A leader's primary task is to get the best possible work out of their team. They need to inspire them to focus on the task at hand, which means being involved in what they're doing, providing support as needed, praising their efforts but setting high standards, and rewarding successes.

- *Communicating the Message*. The leader needs to ensure that their team understands not only what's expected of them, but the big picture as well. Communication is an essential skill for any leader, and the coach can help any individual who is somewhat deficient in that area.

The Leader as Coach

So far in this chapter, we have looked at the benefits of coaching for senior executives. For individuals who want to make the transition to leadership, coaching provides an excellent means for working on those skills in a suitable environment. At the end of this chapter, we will look at some case studies of executives who benefited greatly from coaching to illustrate the potential it has for that group.

Not surprisingly, however, many effective leaders are also excellent coaches themselves. Since one of the key characteristics of a leader is their ability to bring out the best in others, coaching offers an ideal opportunity to hone that particular skill.

Commandment Number Eight:

To become a **real** *leader, to bring out the* **best** *in your people, learn the art of coaching.*

There are three simple reasons why leaders should seriously consider practising the art of coaching:

- *Business Results.* As has been argued throughout this book, today's organisations need to get the best out of their people and coaching is the way to accomplish just that. Effective leaders are people who inspire and encourage others, who bring out the best in the people who work for them. Coaching is an ideal way to develop that kind of loyalty and commitment in the team.

- *Career Advancement.* The individuals who advance in organisations today are the ones who get the best out of their teams or divisions. A leader is only as effective as the people they lead, and coaching is an ideal way to maximise the team's performance.

- *Personal Satisfaction.* When done well, coaching can be an extremely satisfying activity. Leaders looking back on the accomplishments of their careers are most likely to remember the people they helped, not the revenue targets they met or exceeded. To groom someone for greatness, or to help someone deal with a personal crisis, can be the best legacy a leader could want — and coaching can help to achieve it.

Mentor-Coach Case Studies

Below are some case examples of senior executives who have benefited from the mentor-coach process. The problems and solutions described may seem uncomplicated or even obvious, but it is worth noting that in each instance change would not have come about without coaching. The key is that the process forces the individual to face the problem, consider alternatives, and then take action. The mentor-coach's role is to facilitate the process — which in reality is not as easy as it may appear in the examples below! In all cases, the details have been changed to protect privacy.

Case Study A — Managing the Team

This case involves the executive of a large division in a major corporation. He was someone who was very efficient and highly focused, particularly upwards, where there were various major issues to be dealt with. Unfortunately, he was not

*willing or able to expend similar energies on his team below,
which was causing major difficulties. The team was feeling
unappreciated, ignored, unfulfilled and demotivated, and
their job performance had fallen to a dangerously low level.
The executive was aware of the problem but had not taken
any steps to deal with it.*

*The session began with a general "how are things going"
question which was followed by an hour-long discussion of the
pressures he was feeling from above. He was able to get a great
deal off his chest during that time and was visibly less stressed
as a result — indeed, it was an excellent example of the thera-
peutic effects of spilling one's guts to a receptive audience.*

*During a brief pause for a fresh cup of coffee, I then asked
him how things were going with his team. He said that he
honestly didn't know, as he simply hadn't had the time to
manage them properly. I asked him if he was aware of how his
team felt about it and he admitted that he had an idea that they
weren't happy. Some additional discussion confirmed that
there was definitely a problem and we agreed that something
had to be done about it. Eventually, we decided that he would
need to devote a bit of time to some high quality meetings with
his staff. He agreed to one-to-one meetings every two weeks,
quarterly team dinner meetings and formal half-year appraisals. After six months, the situation had improved considerably
and everyone — especially the senior executive — benefited.*

*The key to this case was the relaxed and unthreatening
way in which the discussion evolved. The individual was able
to calmly accept that there was a problem and agree to con-*

sider solutions. If he had been attacked and accused by one of his superiors that he was letting down his team and had better shape up, he very well might have become defensive or try to shift the blame elsewhere. The absence of conflict or criticism allowed for common sense to prevail and a very positive result was achieved.

Case Study B — The Workaholic MD

In this case, the individual being coached was a managing director who was a workaholic. He was single and worked seven days a week quite happily. I was asked to come in as a coach to help him to understand that he simply could not continue working at that pace. He was also getting needlessly involved with responsibilities of his board and other senior management. There was a considerable amount of stress at the top levels of the organisation and it was clear that action was needed.

Although the MD had been asked to come and see me, he was nonetheless in a positive frame of mind. He talked for a long time about his job and it was clear that he was determined to be involved in every aspect of it. Unfortunately, it was also clear that he could not see the wood for the trees and that his preoccupation with the details was preventing him from having a clear view of the whole organisation.

Over several sessions, we talked a great deal about the importance of balance in one's life, about how the most effective leaders also had outside interests that helped to keep them fresh on the job. He agreed whole-heartedly but seemed to think that I was talking about someone else. He even mentioned one member of his team that he had some concerns about and asked me for advice on how he might approach her. Clearly, there were problems here with this MD's self-knowledge and self-awareness.

Eventually, there was little I could do but to speak to him frankly about his work habits. I explained that there was some concern about the hours he was putting in, as well as a problem with board members feeling that he was infringing on their responsibilities. His first reaction was a mixture of surprise and annoyance, but finally he was able to see his situation through the eyes of others and agreed to make some changes. It took him a while to learn how not to be involved in every aspect of the organisation, but over time he was able to sharpen his focus on his own responsibilities and let others get on with theirs. He even took up golf — which allowed him to exchange one fixation for another!

Case Study C — Providing Vision and Direction

Our third case study involves the Owner/Managing Director of a small software company that was undergoing major changes. Sarah had started the company three years before I saw her, and had previously worked for a major computer company in Dublin. Her company developed specialist software products aimed at the health industry and had grown dramatically in a very short period of time.

When Sarah came to me she was looking for advice on what direction the company should take over the next couple of years. She knew that she had to make a decision soon, as the company was at a crossroads and either had to raise serious finance to grow, or else had to merge with one of her competitors, or possibly even be sold outright. Sarah was under considerable strain, as each possibility had its attractions and drawbacks.

I knew very little about the software industry and was obviously not able to give any kind of technical advice. Fortunately, a good coach doesn't need to, as the key is to help the individual explore the options and decide for themselves which one is best. In this case, Sarah was torn between the pressures of running a much larger company versus the possibility of losing control over something that she had built up from scratch. She needed to work through her own priorities and goals — which in this case included a husband and two small children — and try to determine where she wanted to be in five years' time.

We had five sessions together and gradually Sarah was able to weigh all the options and decide what she wanted to do. She realised that her greatest enjoyment came from the creative side of software development and that she didn't really want to run a larger company. She still had a difficult decision to make but at least she was clearer about what she wanted. Eventually, she merged her company with another and was able to focus on creating new products and let someone else manage the day-to-day affairs of the company.

Case Study D — Developing Steeliness at Work

Our final case study involves a very capable manager who was considered too nice to become a truly effective leader in the organisation. While it is thankfully no longer true that one has to be a bit of a bastard to succeed and that "nice guys

finish last", there is something to be said for showing tough-
ness when necessary. More specifically, the team has to know
that the manager cannot be walked on and that he will exert
his authority as needed.

When this manager came to me, he was in line for a pro-
motion but had heard through the grapevine that some of the
directors had major reservations about him. Although he was
an inspirational manager and there was no question about
the quality of his work, there was a belief that he was simply
too nice and would not be able to take tough decisions if
needed.

My client felt that this perception was not particularly
accurate, but realised that he would have to do something to
counteract it. Over a few sessions we discussed the situation
and considered possible solutions. My client was under-
standably reluctant to change his basic management style,
since it was clearly effective, but wanted to find a way to
show that he could be steely when it was called for.

We finally decided that he would try a very simple tech-
nique. The next time he was aware of some sloppy work by a
member of his team, he would let himself get really angry in a
highly public way. I told him that it was OK to lose his tem-
per on occasion as a way of countering his nice guy image.
He even practised beforehand to rehearse what he would say,
using appropriately colourful language.

This simple strategy worked and before long his image had
changed considerably. He eventually went on to a top job in
the organisation.

Chapter Ten

Coaching the Whole Person

In an earlier chapter, we noted that one of the key mistakes coaches make is to focus strictly on an individual's job performance without endeavouring to find out what else is going on in their life. This is true not only when difficulties arise — issues at home, health problems, etc. — but in general it is important to get a complete picture of someone in order to coach them effectively. People are complex beings, and a good coach needs to take a holistic view of each and every one of them.

In my previous book, *The Whole Manager: Achieving Success without Selling Your Soul*, I put great emphasis on the need for business people to have the courage to forget about work on occasion and to spend time with their families, their friends or even themselves. The work would not suffer — in fact, in most cases their job performance would be likely to improve. The response I got to that simple message was overwhelming and highly gratifying. People would come up and say to me, "You mean I don't have to kill myself to get ahead?"

Coaches need to be fully aware of this desire for people to lead full and well-rounded lives. By helping to alleviate the stress people feel at work, by encouraging them to pursue outside interests, to go on holidays with their family, or to give themselves permission to indulge in a bit of relaxation, the coach can accomplish a great deal in this regard. And the place to start is by focusing on the whole person.

Commandment Number Nine:

Remember: You need to coach the
whole *person, not just the employee.*

Background, Family, Beliefs

In order to understand someone, it is very useful to know about their personal history — their family upbringing, their childhood experiences, their educational background, and so on. Typically, this information can be learned during early sessions when rapport is being developed, though sometimes it will come up later when working on specific problems.

Along with their background, it is important to get a sense of their personal beliefs and convictions, possibly including religious and political views and other relatively personal matters. The intention here is not to pry but to gain a better understanding of the whole person. The coach at all times needs to be non-judgemental and to keep their own views firmly in check, especially if they differ substantially from those of the individual. The cardinal rule is always to respect the views of the other, and not to argue with them or try to change them. But if a person has very strong political views, for example, or is deeply involved in a particular organisation outside of work, that information could be very important for the coach at a later date.

Core Values and Self-knowledge

In addition to their personal beliefs, the coach must also get a sense of the individual's core values — that is, the guiding principles by which they live their life. For some, these will stem from their family upbringing, while for others they may be the result of a particularly influential teacher or some other major influence on their thinking. Whatever the source, the coach should have an understanding of what they are. Similarly, the coach needs to get a sense of the extent of the individual's self-knowledge. That is, are these core beliefs deeply felt and immutable, or are they something they simply repeat without thinking? Do they really know what they think and feel, or is there a chance these core beliefs may change? Are there particular barriers or blind spots that are holding them back?

Dreams and Aspirations

The coach should also try to get a sense of what the individual would really like to do with their life. What are their dreams and goals? What is it that drives them? What are the top priorities for them, both in terms of their work and their personal life? What would be their dream come true ten years down the road? For example, if you are spending hours working on someone's career and all they really want to do is be a Shakespearean actor, you could have saved yourself a lot of time and grief by understanding their dreams early on!

Obviously, this whole area can be a sensitive one, so if a coach meets reluctance here it is probably best to move on (see "Privacy Issues" below).

Outside Interests

Most people have numerous outside interests, which are essential for achieving balance and developing the whole person. These can include participating in athletics or on sports teams, being involved in amateur theatre or book reading groups, or possibly doing voluntary work for charities or church groups. In nearly all cases, the coach should encourage such activities and show genuine interest. These outside interests can be very important, particularly for people having difficulty at work, and the coach needs to understand what satisfaction and sense of accomplishment they provide that might be missing elsewhere. For example, an individual who seems afraid to express their views in a business meeting might have no such difficulty in their parents' and teachers' association. The coach needs to then understand what is different and how to respond.

Privacy Issues

In dealing with non-work-related issues, the coach needs to be acutely aware of the individual's right to privacy. Despite the fact that confidentiality has been guaranteed, many individuals will be uncomfortable talking about certain aspects of their lives and the coach obviously should not try to force them to do so. For some, their religious beliefs or political views are private matters and they may feel that they are not relevant to the coaching process. The coach may not agree, but usually will have to accede to their wishes. Other topics that can be clearly off-limits would include sexual preferences, marital difficulties, personal legal problems, and so on. The coach needs to exercise great tact and consideration in broaching personal matters and know when to back off as needed.

The Problem of Time

One of the key dilemmas facing people today is "finding the time". It is often the main complaint in personal relationships, family issues, self-development, leisure pursuits, and so on. Time problems are a major cause of stress and a source of constant frustration for many.

In dealing with the whole person, the coach will usually have to confront this problem of time at some point. I would offer two suggested approaches that many have found enormously successful:

1. ***Think of time as something to be treasured***, in the same way as you would think about your health, personal relationships, financial security and so forth. Time is precious — treat it as such.

2. ***Get organised***. Plan as carefully as possible how you spend your time. Schedule your holidays well in advance, plan your weekends, your leisure time, your time with your family. I don't mean that you have to plan every moment — that would be a bit too regimented and robot-like — but you do need to be aware that time is another resource that has to be used properly.

Any coach who can help an individual get on top of time will have accomplished a great deal — and will be amazed at how other things tend to then fall into place.

Working with Workaholics

Most coaches will have frequent dealings with people who seem to live for their work. They will often have many admirable qualities, such as their dedication, commitment, job performance, determination, and so on, and the coach at first may fail to see a problem. But then tell-tale signs start to emerge, such as the consistent need to work late and on weekends, a certain haggard and dispirited demeanour, etc. and the experienced coach will realise that they are dealing with a workaholic.

There are numerous reasons why someone may become a workaholic — an inability to delegate, feelings of insecurity or inadequacy, problems at home, excessive ambition, and so on — and the coach will need to ascertain the reason in each individual case and help to devise a strategy to deal with it. Often the first step is to convince the individual that there is a problem and that they are doing themselves no favours by working non-stop. Life is short, and the coach needs to persuade the individual that it should be lived to its fullest.

The coach will also be aware that the workaholic usually does the organisation no favours. They tend to have difficulty with team members, are less respected and even disliked, and often develop health or personal problems. Additionally, in my experience such people tend not to see the bigger picture and get tied up with minutiae. For all concerned, the coach needs to help the workaholic become a more well-rounded person.

Balance is the Key

A natural follow-on to the above is the need for balance in all our lives. To my mind, this may be the single most important message a coach can impart to someone. To live a happy and contented life, one must achieve balance — balance between work and home, balance between personal objectives and family life, balance between ambitious goals and realistic expectations, balance between financial rewards and personal satisfaction, and so on. When people lose their sense of balance, when they are willing to step all over others to achieve their goals, or to sacrifice watching their children grow up in order to climb the corporate ladder, it is time to stop and reflect. And this is exactly what a coach can help them to do.

Focus on Fun

Another benefit of coaching, and one often not given serious consideration, is that a coach can help someone to lighten up and enjoy their job more. The workplace can become a very serious and humourless place, which helps to explain the grim expressions seen on Monday mornings and the joyful ones on Friday evenings, and steps need to be taken to put it into perspective. The coach can help people to relax, to see the humorous side of goings on at work and even to laugh at themselves. Again, life is short — enjoy it!

One client I had said that during coaching sessions with his staff he would specifically focus on the fun factor. In both team and one-to-one sessions, he would ask people to rate the fun factor on a scale from one to ten. If it was below seven, then he would ask for ideas on how it could be given a boost.

Understanding the Whole Person

It is simply not possible to coach someone effectively without understanding the whole person — the values, beliefs, opinions, relationships and so forth that makes each person unique. We are all complicated beings, and while there is a tendency to make certain assumptions and to suppose that because a certain strategy worked with "A", it will also work with "B", the reality tends to be not so straightforward. Each person is unique, and each person needs to be seen from different angles to understand what makes them tick.

It is particularly important to be conscious of possible problems outside the job that could be affecting work performance, especially when dealing with a person who is in some difficulty. I was once involved with a highly effective manager who suddenly started to behave a bit oddly. First, he started taking a lot of time off from work due to illness and personal reasons, which was unusual, and then he started coming to work dressed in very flashy suits and sporting a Rolex on his wrist. He was also increasingly distracted at work and his colleagues were becoming concerned. During our coaching session, it finally transpired that his wife had just left him for another man and he was unsurprisingly in some turmoil. By taking a whole person approach, however, I was able to put his behaviour in some perspective and able to offer some advice on his situation.

Chapter Eleven

Coaching is for (Almost) Everyone

We have seen throughout this book that coaching offers many opportunities for development to people in organisations of all kinds. It helps people to learn new skills, deal with problems, build self-esteem, overcome fears and much more. We have also seen how it has potential for people at all levels in the organisation, from new employees just starting out to senior executives with major responsibilities.

In this chapter, we're going to look at coaching outside of the corporation and consider its possibilities for people in all walks of life. Most of the fundamentals remain the same, but different incentives and different relationships will often mean that a somewhat different approach is required.

We're then going to consider some of the reasons why organisations might not be convinced that coaching is right for them. In other words, if the benefits of coaching are so obvious and considerable, why doesn't every organisation practise it?

First, we will look at coaching as it applies to the following groups:

- Non-profit or voluntary organisations
- Small companies
- Community organisations
- Partners and children.

Non-profit or Voluntary Organisations

Many people work in organisations that are based on a different purpose than the corporate profit motive. This would include the civil service, education, health care, social services, police, charity organisations, and so on. For individuals in these professions, issues around personal advancement, reporting relationships, job satisfaction, career options, etc. can be very different than in the corporate sector. For the coach, this can represent both opportunities and difficulties.

A key difference for people in this sector would be one of motivation. For a variety of reasons, financial rewards would be less of a motivating factor for individuals in these areas and their job satisfaction is more likely to come from other sources. In discussing issues around change and growth, therefore, the coach is much more likely to focus on the intrinsic nature of the work and the satisfaction it provides rather than financial compensation.

For example, the advancement possibilities and salary potential for a schoolteacher are relatively limited, but the job satisfaction can be enormous. Equally, however, the frustration and stress can be considerable. The coach would therefore need to focus on what they particularly liked about teaching — why they chose it as a career in the first place — and then discuss the frustrations and consider any options that could alleviate them. As in other coaching situations, the goal would be to build self-esteem and to provide support and whatever assistance is needed.

Coaching would appear to be relatively rare in professions such as teaching, nursing, police work and the civil service, which is unfortunate, as it could provide rich rewards for people working in those fields. Many such people feel undervalued and under-utilised, and a coach could help them to better appreciate their own contributions to society and to deal with the considerable stress that often goes with their jobs. As in the corporate world, people in these sectors are now expected to do more and more, often without adequate resources, and coaching would be one way to increase their productivity, job performance and sense of accomplishment.

Small Companies

Coaching is mostly considered appropriate for large companies with their considerable communication and people management issues. But in reality, coaching can be at least equally effective in very small companies.

We noted earlier that the most important asset any organisation has is its people, and this would be particularly true in the smaller company. A star performer here can make an enormous difference — as can a chronic underachiever.

Small companies also tend to have fewer resources to devote to training and other forms of employee development. This means that they need to find creative ways to get their people up to speed and coaching can provide an ideal opportunity.

Coaching would typically follow a slightly different pattern in the smaller company. The owner would most often be the coach and a close working relationship would usually already be in place. The goal, therefore, would be to focus on skill development and on creating a well-rounded individual. In smaller companies, employees often have many different job responsibilities that require various skills. Coaching is an ideal way to identify what is needed and the best way to acquire it.

Some owner-managers are likely to complain that they simply don't have the time to devote to coaching, and one does have to be sympathetic to the pressures small business owners are under. On the other hand, many small businesses fail because they have not adequately developed key personnel and I would suggest that they need to find the time if they want their companies to survive and prosper.

In the Community

In this book we have mainly looked at coaching in a business context, but there are many other instances where coaching could be beneficial. In fact, in any situation where advice or information is transmitted on a one-to-one basis, the fundamentals of coaching could be extremely useful. Here would be a few non-business applications of coaching principles:

- *Community outreach agencies.* For those people working in voluntary agencies of various kinds, coaching can be a great help to them in managing and developing those for whom they are responsible. Whether it's working with disadvantaged youth, senior citizens, disabled people or recent immigrants, the basic principles of coaching — collaborative process in a non-judgemental environment, problem-solving ethos, partnership approach, and so on — would have considerable potential for helping people in a supportive way.

- *Youth Organisations.* Similar to the above, many people work in their spare time with the Boy Scouts, Junior Achievement groups or other youth associations to help young people develop. Coaching skills could be very effective with these groups, as it teaches them to be more self-reliant and confident.

- *Friends and neighbours.* Coaching fundamentals can also be useful in helping friends or neighbours deal with personal or work-related problems. It would not necessarily be labelled "coaching", but the kind of advice given and the approach taken could still be the same as in a formal coaching session.

- *Sports teams.* Here the connection with coaching is obvious, but it's still worth noting the benefits of one-to-one coaching in the development of athletic and interpersonal skills.

Partners and Children

The principles of coaching could also be used in one's relationship with a partner or children. Again, it need not be labelled as "coaching", but the basic principles such as collaboration, respect, empathy, helping others to help themselves, etc. all have clear application in personal relationships as well. Most successful marriages would include numerous instances where one partner acted as a "coach" to the other, and the advantages of coaching in terms of child-rearing should be fairly obvious.

Reasons for Not Coaching

Since throughout this book we have extolled the virtues of coaching, it's worth considering why every organisation doesn't put it at the heart of their management development programme. Below are some possible reasons why some organisations might resist coaching:

Time and Expense

By far the biggest drawback to coaching for most people would be that it is a time-consuming process and time is a precious commodity. There is some truth to this complaint, as coaching sessions do take time and must be scheduled as another task in the busy working day. Readers will not be surprised, however, that I would argue that in the long run coaching *saves* time as it helps people be more effective and prioritised.

Privacy Issues, Not Comfortable with Process

Some people might feel that coaching is intrusive and that people would not be comfortable talking about themselves with someone else, especially their direct supervisor. Or they might feel that coaching is *too* personal and thus inappropriate. As has been discussed earlier, privacy and confidentiality are important issues in the coaching process and need to be respected for it to succeed. As coaching becomes more common, however, its fundamental components will be known to all and these problems are less likely to arise.

Too Loose and Unstructured

Organisations and managers used to a top-down, command-and-control structure may find coaching too unstructured for their liking. They tend to prefer that management be in charge and employees be told what to do. As we saw in the first chapter, however, such management structures are less effective in today's economy, as they do not get the best possible work out of people.

Preference for, and Commitment to, Other Forms of Development

Many organisations have invested heavily in expensive training and development programmes for their managers and employees. Whether it be for time management skills or stress reduction strategies, these programmes can become entrenched in organisations and top management might assume that they are already doing all they need to in this area. The problem, of course, is that many of these programmes are largely ineffective and limited in their scope. They are not tailored to the individual needs of employees and can only offer a packaged solution in specific areas. The issues facing people today are complex and personal, and standard programmes are simply not adequate. Also, one-to-one coaching is a much more effective method of learning specific skills or abilities than any other form of training.

Lack of Awareness, Apathy, Dislike of Change

For many organisations, coaching has simply not occurred to them or not been considered because it's "too much trouble". These organisations may be happy with the status quo, although I would argue that the benefits of coaching are so clear that many such organisations will eventually come around to it.

Chapter Twelve

The Ten Commandments of Coaching

As a useful way of summarising some of the ideas in this book, this chapter lists my Ten Commandments of Coaching with a brief discussion on each. Readers may very well come up with their own commandments, and if so, I would welcome receiving them!

1. Stop just managing — coaching is the key to success in today's organisations.

The nature of business has changed dramatically in recent years, but unfortunately the way we manage people has not. Today's organisations need people who are innovative, committed, team players, devoted to learning, risk-takers, excellent communicators, flexible and balanced. These qualities cannot be nurtured by traditional top-down, command-and-control organisations. Companies that still operate that way simply will not get the best out of their people.

Coaching can bring out remarkable changes in individuals. Barriers and blockages to success are removed, people feel they are valued and integral parts of the organisation, and specific problems or weaknesses can be worked on in a supportive and safe environment. The entire culture of a company will improve as communication is improved and mutual trust developed. It is not surprising that people who receive one-to-one coaching are more productive, more content and more likely to be loyal to the organisation.

2. Coaching means helping others to help themselves — if it's not a collaborative process, it's not coaching.

One of the fundamentals of coaching is that the coach is there to help guide the process, but real change and improvement can only come through the efforts of the individuals themselves. Educators have long realised that people learn much better when they discover things for themselves, rather than being told by others. Coaching works on the same principle. Telling someone how to respond to a problem is not nearly as effective as guiding them towards the solution on their own.

In coaching sessions, the onus is squarely on the individual to consider the issues at hand and any possible responses. This in effect puts them in control over their fate, and prevents them from being over-dependent on others. The coach can help by asking penetrating questions and challenging the person if they are avoiding certain issues, but to be successful the individual must feel that they have found the correct course of action themselves.

3. Confidentiality is key — lose their trust and "the game is over".

Quite simply, coaching is built on trust. To be successful, coaching requires an honest and revealing exchange of views where nearly any and all issues can be discussed. Due to painful past experiences, many people are quite wary of being completely candid in such discussions, which can make progress slow or impossible. The answer to this problem is for the coach to give an ironclad guarantee of confidentiality and then to live up to it.

This guarantee of confidentiality is one of the aspects that makes coaching both unique and effective. In any other type of one-to-one intervention the manager is likely to be spouting a company line and the employee is likely to be saying whatever they think the manager wants to hear. In coaching, the individual can express an honest opinion and the coach will respect it and they can both move on from there.

4. Establishing rapport is an absolutely essential coaching skill.

Rapport can be defined as a "sympathetic relationship or understanding with another" which is obviously a key skill for any coach. The coach must not only have a sincere interest in others, but also be able to see things from their point of view. Coaching is always about the individual being coached, and the coach must be able to put aside their own views and assumptions to focus on those of the individual.

Rapport can take on different forms and be expressed in different ways, but it must be experienced mutually to actually be rapport. The coach and the individual must be comfortable with each other, have mutual respect and approach the sessions with good intentions. They don't have to agree or see eye-to-eye, but they do have to *understand* each other to be able to make progress.

5. There is no one right way to coach — different people and different situations require different approaches.

Coaching would be much simpler if there were a single set of rules to follow to get the desired results. People are far too complicated for that and instead the coach must be able to adapt their style and message to the situation at hand. Some people are very inner-directed and just need to be pointed in the right direction; others lack motivation or confidence and need a more active approach. The good coach will be part psychologist, part teacher, part drill instructor, and part confidante, as the situation requires. The key, again, is to understand the individual being coached and the approach that will bring out the best in that person.

6. Coaching can also be very effective upwards and sideways in the organisation.

Most people think of coaching as typically occurring downwards in an organisation — that is, from a more senior person to a more junior one — but that need not necessarily be the case. Because coaching is based on collaboration and mutual respect, coaching can also be effective upwards and sideways in the organisation. A particularly secure senior manager would have no difficulty being coached by a subordinate, as a fresh and different view could be extremely useful. Similarly, colleagues who are at the same level in the organisation can benefit from coaching in certain circumstances, for example, to learn specific skills or benefit from another's experiences. The key, as in all coaching interventions, is that an honest and confidential exchange take place in a safe and supportive environment.

7. In times of personal or organisational turbulence, coaching can be an absolute godsend.

When things go wrong, or major disruptive change occurs, the benefits of coaching are more apparent than ever. In non-coaching organisations, individuals are typically left on their own when crises strike. In a coaching environment, however, the individual undergoing major change has someone to talk to and confide in. The coach will be able to offer comfort, advice, support or whatever is needed to help the situation.

Coaching during times of turbulence is not only a godsend for the individual, but also for the organisation. Employees who are under pressure — either due to problems at work or at home — do not perform anywhere near their capability, which has repercussions for their colleagues and the organisation as a whole. Coaching can get them back on the rails more quickly.

8. To become a *real* leader, to bring out the *best* in your people, learn the art of coaching.

Coaching is not just for the Human Resource Department and is not only appropriate for individuals with specific problems or challenges. Coaching is a powerful tool that can help anyone become a leader others will want to follow. It can help to develop loyalty, to convince people to put in that extra effort, to inspire them to do great things. Above all, coaching can help to bring out the best in people — which is, after all, what a leader is paid to do.

Coaching can also help leaders improve their own skills and effectiveness, to bring out the best in themselves. In the fast-paced and competitive economy of today, effective leadership is essential for companies to survive and prosper, and coaching can help to bring out the leader in anyone.

9. Remember: you need to coach the *whole* person, not just the employee.

People are complicated beings and they don't shed their personal lives when they walk through the company door. Each person has their own dreams, aspirations, fears, worries, beliefs and so on, and to coach them effectively, it is important to understand what makes them tick. This doesn't mean prying into their personal lives or asking them embarrassing questions, but it does mean taking an interest in the non-work-related aspects of their lives. It makes no sense spending hours trying to convince someone that they need to be less distracted at work, when in reality they have a sick child at home that they are worried to death about. Coaches must deal with the *whole* person.

10. Coaching is for (almost) everyone — managers, parents, teachers, you and me.

The benefits of coaching are not restricted to a few senior people in large organisations. The principles apply to people at all levels, and in organisations of all sizes. They are equally effective outside of the business world. In youth organisations, community groups, with friends and family, the fundamentals of coaching can be extremely useful in dealing with problems, developing skills and confidence and much more.

There are a variety of reasons why organisations do not introduce a coaching programme — from a preference for other forms of development to a dislike of the egalitarian ethos of coaching to outright apathy and lack of awareness — but any organisation that is serious about developing its people to their fullest potential should consider its potential. Coaching may not be a magic cure-all for every organisation's ills, but I would argue strongly that there is no better way to get the best out of your team and yourself than through the practice of coaching.

Coaching in Action: The Case of the Underachieving Manager

Kate was sitting at her desk preparing for her first coaching session with one of her managers, Robert. She had mixed feelings about the meeting, as on one hand Robert had the potential to become one of the star performers of the company — something they desperately needed if they were to continue to grow — while on the other hand she knew that he was performing well below his potential. He had plenty of confidence and was very talented, but he was somewhat lazy and abrasive and seemed to have little idea as to how he was perceived by others. He got along fairly well with most people on the team, but could be very impatient with anyone who disagreed with him and always seemed to know best. Kate knew that coaching was either going to bring out the best in Robert — or Robert just might be moving on elsewhere.

"Good morning, Robert, come on in. I'm glad you agreed to start these coaching sessions and I look forward to discussing a few things. Should we go get a coffee before we start?"

"Sounds good."

"How's your wife enjoying her new job? Has she settled in OK?"

"She's doing great, thanks. It's been a big change but she seems to be coping pretty well."

After a few more minutes of general discussion, Kate got down to the business at hand.

"Robert, as you know, we have started a new initiative here to introduce coaching for all managers in the organisation. With the marketplace becoming increasingly competitive we need to get the best possible performance out of all of us and we've decided that individual coaching seems the best way to do so . . ."

Kate then described the fundamentals of coaching and together they set the ground rules for the first and subsequent sessions. She asked Robert if it would be OK if she asked her colleagues for their impressions of him in general, and for any areas he might improve on in particular. She said that since he was somebody with potential to rise in the company, this information would be useful for both of them. Robert was more than willing to agree and said that he was looking forward to the meetings.

Kate was a firm believer that perceptions of people were very nearly as important as actual results, especially when it came to advancement in the company. She knew of numerous instances of promotions that occurred based more on how the individuals were viewed than on what they had actually accomplished. It was this idea of perception that she knew would be one of the main topics of her sessions with Robert.

At the next meeting, Kate began by emphasising Robert's strengths that had consistently appeared in his appraisals. She noted that he had completed several projects very successfully and in general had been praised for the quality of his work. She asked him for some ideas on how some of his strengths could be further developed and they agreed on some specific points that became part of the action plan.

Kate then moved on to a discussion of the responses she received from colleagues concerning Robert and in particular areas where improvements could be made. She explained to him how important she felt that these perceptions were, and that they were something that needed to be worked on.

"Basically, Robert, the response I got from people was that you come across as someone who thinks he knows it all, who was never wrong and who loves the sound of your own voice. Several people mentioned that you are not particularly receptive to the ideas of others and not a good team player."

Robert was somewhat taken aback by these comments, but unfortunately there were more.

"In addition, people seem to think that you can do good work if a project particularly interests you, but that you were much less likely to get stuck in on projects you found boring or simply didn't like. The general feeling was that you are nowhere near living up to your potential and that in fact you can be a bit lazy. Finally, there was a sense that you are somewhat arrogant and feel superior to the other members of the team."

"But I don't think that's fair," Robert said. "It sounds to me like you're describing someone else altogether. I honestly don't feel that any of those things are true. Besides, are you just going to take their word for it? What about all those positive things in my appraisals?"

"I understand all that, Robert, but the point is that people have those perceptions of you and I think it's something we need to work on. These sessions are not about finding fault, nor are they just another form of appraisal. They are intended to help you to build on your strengths and to find strategies for dealing with any shortcomings. One of the ways to do that is to solicit the views of others to get an honest appraisal of your work performance. Remember: perception can be reality."

Robert thought for a moment and then said, "Fine, I understand that I need to work well with others, but I still don't think they know the real me. Maybe I can be a little bit impatient sometimes, but you said yourself that we're under a lot of pressure and I'm just trying to get things done."

"That's fair enough, Robert, and please believe that no one is rushing to judgement here. The point is that how you are perceived by others is important and it's something that together we can work on. But it's by no means the only thing we're going to discuss during these sessions. I want to know what kind of challenges and frustrations you're facing, what kind of support you need from me and others, what your long-term goals are and whatever else you want to talk about. These sessions are as much for you as they are for me and the

organisation in general, and I hope that after a while you'll actually be looking forward to them."

Robert eventually realised the wisdom of what Kate was saying and agreed to work on various issues, including how he was perceived by others. They started by Kate asking him how he would like to be perceived.

"I'd like to be thought of as someone who is rational and interested in focusing on all the top priorities. A team player who seeks advice from others and is prepared to take on any ideas better than my own. A strong self-motivator who gets things done but who has no difficulty getting on with his colleagues."

With this ideal perception in mind — which was markedly different from the perception others seemed to hold — Kate and Robert began working on specific ways that would help to improve the situation.

Over time, Robert was able to learn how to be a better listener and less judgmental of the suggestions of others. He made a conscious effort to involve others whenever he could and to place greater emphasis on everyday courtesy and showing respect to whomever he was addressing. Above all, he developed a new mindset of being a team player and putting the interests and accomplishments of the group above his own.

After several months of coaching sessions, Kate felt that Robert had changed and once again solicited the views of others about his attitude and performance. She was delighted that across the board a definite improvement had been noted.

When Kate told Robert that how he was perceived in the organisation had taken a noticeable turn for the better, he looked at her and said, somewhat mischievously, "See, I told you those things were untrue."

Kate just smiled and once again congratulated herself on introducing coaching to the team.